Delivering Quality in the NHS 2005

Edited by

Professor Sir Michael Rawlins

Chairman
National Institute for Health and Clinical Excellence

and

Professor Peter Littlejohns

Clinical Director
National Institute for Health and Clinical Excellence

Radcliffe Publishing
Oxford • Seattle

Radcliffe Publishing Ltd
18 Marcham Road
Abingdon
Oxon OX14 1AA
United Kingdom

www.radcliffe-oxford.com
The Radcliffe Publishing electronic catalogue and online ordering facility.
Direct sales to anywhere in the world.

British Library Cataloguing in Publication Data

A catalogue record for this book is available from the British Library.

ISBN 1 85775 742 4

Typeset by Acorn Bookwork, Salisbury, Wiltshire
Printed and bound by TJ International Ltd, Padstow, Cornwall

Contents

List of contributors   vii

List of abbreviations   x

Introduction   xiii

Part One: Research and development   1

The new R&D agenda: the NHS contribution   3
Sally Davies

Navigating the new regulations   6
Janet H Darbyshire

The future focus of public health research   9
Mike Kelly

Putting clinical research into practice   13
Kirstine Knox and David J Kerr

Effective ways for implementing research in a clinical environment:
benefits, barriers and future challenges   17
Adrian Davis

Research ethics: a barrier or gateway to quality research?   20
Simon Woods

Part Two: Striving for excellence   25

Looking backwards to the future   27
Michael D Rawlins

Measuring what matters: a new approach to assessment   32
Anna Walker

Part Three: Commissioning for quality in mental health   37

Commissioning mental health services   39
Alan Cohen

Commissioning quality in mental health   43
Janet Millar

Part Four: James Lind Alliance: identifying patients' and clinicians'
priorities for therapeutic research   47

No commercial potential? (nullus pretii)   49
Frank Arnold

Therapeutic research into psoriasis: patients' perspectives, priorities
and interests   53
Ray Jobling

Involving the public in health technology assessment   57
Sandy Oliver

Identifying patients' and clinicians' priorities in cancer clinical trials   62
Hazel Thornton

Part Five: Getting governance right   67

Do NHS structural issues hamper R&D?   69
Marc Taylor

Audit: does it work and is it worth the effort?   73
John Holden

How new regulatory structures underpin accountability within
integrated and multidisciplinary teams: the role of CHRE   77
Julie Stone

The impact of stakeholders on the NICE guideline development process   81
Henny Pearmain

Part Six: Developing and implementing NICE guidance   85

The Health Technology Assessment Programme: supporting NICE   87
Tom Walley

Disseminating a psychological treatment for eating disorders   91
Christopher G Fairburn

Improvement Partnership for Ambulance Services: what we do and
how we do it   95
Julia RA Taylor

Implementing pressure ulcer guidance: a success story   99
Menna Lloyd-Jones and Trudie Young

Implementing head injury guidance   103
A David Mendelow

Implementation of NICE guidance: an ABPI perspective   106
David Brickwood

Measuring the impact of NICE guidance across 28 disease areas   110
Simon Howard

Audit into the implementation of NICE guidance for Roche drugs   119
Paul Catchpole

Part Seven: Achieving quality in public health   125

Preventing falls in older people   127
Maurice Wilson

Public health, primary care and quality   130
Andrew Scott-Clark

Developing the 'smokefree hospital'   134
Bryan Stoten

Part Eight: Patient safety and clinical risk   139

Implementing guidance of safe medication practice   141
David Cousins

The miracle of the general practice consultation   144
Roger Neighbour

Local implementation of new interventional procedures   147
Barrie D White

Improving the introduction of new interventional procedures: the
Leicester experience   152
Keith Blanshard

Involving clinicians in risk management   154
John HB Scarpello

Management of a major incident in hospital: how theory was put
into practice   157
Brijendra Shravat

Part Nine: Patient focus   161

Chronic disease management: working together to improve patient care –
the practice perspective   163
Roger Gadsby

Evaluation of the Citizens Council of NICE   167
Elizabeth Barnett, Celia Davies, Margie Wetherell and Sarah Seymour-Smith

Patients as drivers for implementation   170
Yvonne Boughton

Evaluating patient and carer involvement in NICE's Clinical Guidelines   174
Victoria Thomas

**Experience as a carer on the NICE self-harm guideline development
group**   178
Richard Pacitti

Index   183

List of contributors

Frank Arnold, Managing Director, Polymed Therapeutics Limited

Dr Elizabeth Barnett, Open University Research Team

Dr Keith Blanshard MBBS FRCR, Chair New Interventional Procedures Advisory Group UHL, Assistant Medical Director (Clinical Effectiveness)

Yvonne Boughton, Secretary/Trustee, FREED

David Brickwood, Vice President of Government Affairs, Johnson and Johnson and the Association of the British Pharmaceutical Industry

Dr Paul Catchpole, Healthcare Management Director, Roche Products Limited

Alan Cohen, Clinical Director of Kensington and Chelsea PCT and Director of Primary Care, Sainsbury Centre for Mental Health

Professor David Cousins, Head of Safe Medication Practice, National Patient Safety Agency

Professor Celia Davies, Open University Research Team

Janet H Darbyshire, OBE, Director, MRC Clinical Trials Unit

Professor Sally Davies, Director of Research and Development, Department of Health

Adrian Davis, MRC Hearing and Communication Group, School of Psychological Sciences, Faculty of Medicine, Dentistry and Nursing, Manchester University

Christopher G Fairburn, Oxford University Department of Psychiatry

Roger Gadsby, GP and Senior Lecturer in Primary Care, University of Warwick

Ray Jobling, Chairman, The Psoriasis Association

Professor Mike Kelly Director of Evidence and Guidance, Health Development Agency

Professor David J Kerr, CBE, Professor of Cancer Therapeutics and Clinical Pharmacology, Director, National Translational Cancer Research Network

John Holden, General Practitioner, St Helens, and Chairman, RCGP 'Fellowship by Assessment'

Simon Howard, Managing Director, Abacus International

Kirstine Knox, Deputy Director, National Translational Cancer Research Network

Menna Lloyd-Jones, Senior Nurse Tissue Viability, North West Wales NHS Trust

Professor A David Mendelow, Head of Department of Neurosurgery, Newcastle General Hospital

Dr Janet Millar, Mendip PCT

Roger Neighbour, President, Royal College of General Practitioners

Sandy Oliver, Reader in Public Policy, Institute of Education, University of London

Richard Pacitti, Chief Executive, MIND

Henny Pearmain, Chair, Clinical Effectiveness Forum for Allied Health Professions

Professor Sir Michael D Rawlins, Chairman, National Institute for Clinical Excellence

Dr John H B Scarpello, University Hospital of North Staffordshire NHS Trust, Stoke on Trent

Andrew Scott-Clark, Director of Public Health, Swale PCT

Dr Sarah Seymour-Smith, Open University Research Team

Brijendra Shravat, Consultant and Lead Clinician in A&E, Barnet Chase Farm Hospital NHS Trust

Julie Stone, Deputy Director, CHRE

Bryan Stoten, Chair, University Hospitals Coventry and Warwickshire NHS Trust and Co-Director, Tobacco Control Collaborating Centre

Marc Taylor, Head of Research Policy & Governance, Department of Health

Julia R A Taylor, National Programme Director, Improvement Partnership for Ambulance Trusts

Victoria Thomas, Assistant Director Patient Involvement Unit, National Institute for Clinical Excellence

Hazel Thornton, Honorary Visiting Fellow, Department of Health Sciences, University of Leicester. Foundation Chair: Consumers' Advisory Group for Clinical Trials (CAG-CT)

Anna Walker, Chief Executive, Healthcare Commission

Professor Tom Walley, Director Heath Technology Assessment Programme

Professor Margie Wetherell, Open University Research Team

Barrie D White, Assistant Medical Director, University Hospital, Queen's Medical Centre, Nottingham

Maurice Wilson, Primary Care Development Trust, Northampton

Simon Woods, Director of Learning Policy Ethics and Life Sciences Research Institute (PEALS)

Trudie Young, Lecturer in Tissue Viability, University of Wales, Bangor

List of abbreviations

ARMD	age-related macular degeneration
ATLS	advanced trauma life support
BPI	British Pharmaceutical Index
CAG-CT	Consumers' Advisory Group for Clinical Trials
CASE	Clinical Audit, Standards and Effectiveness
CBT	cognitive behaviour therapy
CD	clinical director
CEFAHP	Clinical Effectiveness Forum for Allied Health Professions
CGC	Clinical Governance Committee
CHI	Commission for Health Improvement
CHRE	Council for Healthcare Regulatory Excellence
CMO	Chief Medical Officer
CNST	Clincial Negligence Scheme for Trusts
COPD	chronic obstructive pulmonary disease
CPD	continuing professional development
CT	computed tomography
DH	Department of Health
DNA	did not attend
DSN	diabetes specialist nurse
ED	emergency department
EDA	Eating Disorders Association
FDA	Food and Drug Administration
GCP	good clinical practice
GDC	General Dental Council
GDG	Guideline Development Groups
GMAS	Greater Manchester Ambulance Service
GMS	General Medical Services
GSCC	General Social Care Council
HCC	hospital control centre
HDA	Health Development Agency
HPA	Hospital pharmacy audit
HTA	health technology assessment
IB	incapacity benefit
IPAS	Improvement Partnership for Ambulance Services
IPG	Interventional Procedure Guidance
IT	information technology
ITU	intensive therapy unit

IWL	improving working lives
LREC	Local Research Ethics Committee
MA	Modernisation Agency
MAAGS	Medical Audit Advisory Groups
MAT	moving annual totals
MHAS	modernising hearing aid services
MHRA	Medicines and Healthcare products Regulatory Agency
MICT	major incident control team
MIO	medical incident officer
MMT	mobile medical team
MND	motor neurone disease
MRC	Medical Research Council
MREC	Multi-centre Research Ethics Committee
NCAA	National Clinical Assessment Authority
NCC	National Collaborating Centre
NCRI	National Cancer Research Institute
NCRN	National Cancer Research Network
NEAT	new and emerging technologies
NHL	non-Hodgkin's lymphoma
NHS	National Health Service
NICE	National Institute for Clinical Excellence
NIPAG	New Interventional Procedures Advisory Group
NPSA	National Patient Safety Agency
NSF	National Service Framework
NTRAC	National Translational Cancer Research Network
PALS	Patient Advice and Liaison Service
PASI	Psoriasis Area and Severity Index
PCR	polymerase chain reaction
PCT	Primary Care Trust
PDSA	plan, do, study, act
PIU	Patient Involvement Unit
PLDH	pegylated liposomal doxorubicin hydrochloride
PMS	personal medical services
PPP	private public partnership
QAA	Quality Assurance Agency
QEPOD	QMC Enquiry into Patient Outcomes and Deaths
QOF	Quality and Outcomes Framework
R&D	research and development
RAE	Research Assessment Exercise
RCP	Royal College of Physicians
RCT	randomised controlled trial
REC	Research Ethics Committee
SDO	service delivery and organisation
SERNIP	Safety and Efficacy Register of New Interventional Procedures
SHA	Strategic Health Authority

SLA	service level agreement
SXR	skull X-ray
TAR	technology assessment report
UKCRC	UK Clinical Research Collaboration
WDC	Workforce Development Confederation
WTE	whole time equivalent

Introduction

These are the conference proceedings from *Clinical Excellence 2004*. This was the sixth Annual NICE Conference and the last in its 'old' form. From 1 April 2005 the Institute will have responsibility for developing guidance for the public health community which will, inevitably, change the shape of future Annual Conferences.

A key aim of *Clinical Excellence 2004* was to give delegates the opportunity to share best practice and the event brought together a diverse group of people, involved in healthcare, who are responsible for raising standards in the NHS and for implementing best practice. The programme included numerous examples of local projects that have improved service provision and patient care, including sessions on achieving excellence in clinical risk management, service user led services in mental health, and choice as a driver for quality.

This publication brings together papers from many of those who spoke at the conference. It offers delegates the opportunity to refresh their memories and, for those who couldn't attend, a chance to sample some of the outstanding contributions that occurred during the event. These papers offer examples of the type of best practice that goes on throughout the NHS all the time. They demonstrate the excellence of the work undertaken by health professionals and academics who concern themselves with delivering quality and improving patient care. Many of the projects described can be adapted and applied at a local level.

The 2006 conference will build upon the strong reputation that Clinical Excellence has developed whilst reflecting the Institute's new responsibilities and focus. Although the Institute will become the National Institute for Health and Clinical Excellence it will remain known – universally – as NICE.

NICE 2005: Health and Clinical Excellence will take place at the ICC in Birmingham 7–8 December. We look forward to seeing you.

Michael Rawlins
Chairman, NICE

PART ONE

Research and development

The new R&D agenda: the NHS contribution

Sally Davies

NHS R&D was established to provide the evidence on which to base improvements in the health of individuals and the management of disease. Initially the National Programmes funded a series of disease-themed time-related programmes including cancer, primary/secondary care interface and child health. However, it soon became clear that those areas without specific programmes were not able to compete successfully for funds for applied research. The National R&D Programme was therefore changed to support programmes of Health Technology Assessment (HTA), Service Delivery and Organisation (SDO), New and Emerging Technologies (NEAT) and to give increasing support to systematic reviews and research synthesis including the international Cochrane Collaborative groups in England, the Centre for Reviews and Dissemination at York University and the evaluation groups now supporting the work programme of NICE.

Patient-related research including promotion of health, prevention of ill health as well as healthcare delivery, interventions and systems have increasingly been recognised internationally as difficult research areas. Academic excellence from many disciplines is required to collaborate with practitioners and patients; all this as society changes and the public rightly demands increased information and roles in every stage of the healthcare process including research. In addition to complexity, other threats to clinical research are the undervaluing by the healthcare community of the collaboration roles essential to delivering big clinical trials and other well-designed studies and the lack of capacity in the trained research workforce.

In the UK, two reports published in October 2003 highlighted the essential need to build on the strength of the NHS for clinical research by developing new structures, systems and incentives. These reports[1,2] both highlighted the lack of NHS R&D funding to support clinical research as well as the need to improve the regulatory environment and develop national clinical research networks. Further drivers for change adding to the clinical research momentum of the NHS are the report of the Pharmaceutical Industry Competitiveness Task-force[3] work, Sir Derek Wanless' reports[4] to the Treasury, respecting public health and interventions that promote or aim to maintain health as well as the introduction of the research governance. In particular, the health industries, including pharmaceutical companies, biotechnology and healthcare industries, all lobbied hard for improved clinical trials capacity within the NHS in order to allow them to undertake studies of all phases (1, 2, 3 and 4) in the NHS with NHS patients.

Ministers responded by asking Sir John Pattison, as National R&D Director, to chair the Research for Patient Benefit Working Party, which reported in April 2004.[5] This working party recommended to the Government the establishment of a UK Clinical Research Collaboration (UKCRC) to oversee the extension of research infrastructure in the NHS (both experimental medicine and trials), the coordinated funding of research studies, a constructive approach to the coordination and development of research career pathways and the development of 'better regulation' practices. The proposal was accepted by the Government who announced, in the budget of March 2004 additional funding of an extra £25m in 2004/05, rising by £25m each year to an annual total of £100m, over and above inflation added to the NHS R&D budget to develop clinical research.

The NHS R&D budget funds direct research projects through the National Programmes, Trust R&D programmes and in addition, the NHS support costs of clinical research undertaken by our partners such as the Medical Research Council (MRC), Wellcome Trust and the Association of Medical Research Charities. This 'Support for Science' budget pays for the extra diagnostics and healthcare facility use related to the research studies as well as for the NHS governance and management of clinical research. This funding can contribute also to research infrastructure such as equipment, space, trained staff and computing. Clearly, research projects and programmes are funded competitively following peer review to include the expenses of protocol, development, sponsorship, data collection, analysis and write-up.

The new funding is supporting a new National Coordinating Centre for Clinical Research and clinical networks in the areas of mental health, diabetes, medicines for children, stroke and Alzheimer's disease in addition to the existing cancer network. We plan a responsive grant scheme to answer questions arising out of professional practice in the NHS, an increase in post masters level research training as well as supporting the experimental medicine facilities set up by partner funders, in particular the Wellcome Trust.

All of these initiatives will either be led by the UKCRC or worked up in association with partners of the UKCRC. The guiding principles of the UKCRC are to:

- engage stakeholders through consultation and negotiations rather than representation
- adopt a 'solution-based' rather than 'recommendations-based' approach to problems
- build on what is already working well
- improve communication but not at the cost of momentum

- add value by not taking on issues easily tackled by a single partner organisation.

In addition to building up the infrastructure and coordinating research funding in clinical research the UKCRC will assist us all in building up our research workforce, working with the NHS and Department of Health (DH) to build incentives for research in the NHS and developing best practice to streamline the regulatory and governance processes.

The key and potentially unique role of the NHS in clinical research has been recognised by Government, industry and academics; and we are entering an exciting era for clinical research with increased funding and changing structures. I believe the NHS and patients will respond positively and collaborate in more research studies if it is made easy for them. We need to deliver studies to time and of high quality and then it is very probable that yet more funding will be made available.

References

1   Academy of Medical Sciences (2003) *Strengthening Clinical Research* www.acmedsci.ac.uk.

2   Department of Health, BIA & Department of Trade and Industry (2003) *The BIGT Report – Bioscience 2015: Improving national health, increasing national wealth.* www.dti.gov.uk/bio-igt/bio-igt-index.html

3   ABPI (2003) PICTF Report. www.abpi.org.uk/publications/pdfs/78324-doh-pictf-indicators.pdf

4   HM Treasury (2004) *Securing Good Health for the Whole Population Index.* www.hm-treasury.gov.uk./consultations_and_legislation/wanless/consult_wanless03_index.cfm

5   Department of Health (2004) *Research for Patient Benefit Working Party.* www.dh.gov.uk/PolicyAndGuidance/ResearchAndDevelopment/ResearchAndDevelopmentAZ/PrioritiesForResearch/fs/en?CONTENT_ID = 4082668&chk = xUzx/B

Navigating the new regulations

Janet H Darbyshire

The regulatory and governance environment for clinical research in the UK is both complex and changing rapidly. Over the past few years everyone involved in clinical research, including investigators, funders and managers of research in Trusts or universities, has had to understand and adapt to the requirements of the Data Protection Act 1998, Section 60 of the Health and Social Care Act 2001, the NHS Research Governance Framework (2001), the EU Clinical Trials Directive 2001/20/EC (2001) and the regulations implementing the Directive into UK law (2004). In the near future, the Human Tissue Act and the Mental Incapacity Bill are expected to be enacted, both of which have implications for clinical research, and new European regulations on medicinal products for children have been proposed. In addition, other bodies such as the General Medical Council (GMC) have published guidance on consent (1998) and confidentiality (2004), which must also be taken into account. No one would disagree with the underlying objectives of the regulations and guidelines, which are to protect patients and improve the quality and safety of research, but together they form a complex web of requirements which are often duplicative; sometimes conflicting, and which threaten research that could lead to improvements in health.

For those involved in clinical trials, the EU Clinical Trials Directive has had the most profound effect. The Directive, which was published in 2001 and was implemented into UK law in May 2004, regulates the conduct of all clinical trials of medicinal products for human use in the European Union. It covers all phases of trials, from healthy volunteer studies to comparisons of standard treatments using licensed medicines. The aims of the Directive are to protect the rights, safety and well-being of trial participants; and to simplify and harmonise the administrative provisions governing clinical trials in the EU. Although the Directive includes both commercial and non-commercial research, including trials of marketed products, it was primarily intended for the harmonisation of regulations governing trials leading to a marketing authorisation. Regulatory authorities and the pharmaceutical industry were therefore included in discussions with the European Commission, but non-commercial organisations were not involved until very late in the process.

In February 2003 draft regulations to transpose the Directive into UK law were published for consultation with a 12-week period for responses. The MRC, in partnership with the DH, Cancer Research UK, the National Cancer Research Network and academic trialists, undertook an assessment of the impact of the regulations on publicly funded trials, under the Chairmanship of Professor Stephen Evans.

Six key concerns were identified:

- the requirement for a single sponsor, is not compatible with the collaborative approach to sharing of responsibilities in most publicly funded research
- the introduction of rigid approaches to trial monitoring and pharmacovigilance would not be appropriate in many trials of marketed products
- a potentially burdensome and duplicative authorisation process
- requirements for consent by a legal representative for incapacitated individuals would seriously impede recruitment to trials in emergency settings
- lack of clarity over the transitional arrangements for ongoing trials
- increased costs of conducting trials which, in view of limited public funds, would inevitably result in fewer trials.

The impact assessment and other responses from the academic community were taken into account in the redrafting of the UK regulations, particularly in relation to the issue of sponsorship, but a number of concerns remained. In response to these, the MRC and the DH established a Joint Project to codify good practice in publicly funded trials in July 2003. The objectives were to provide practical advice and examples of good practice for all those involved in non-commercial trials to ensure compliance with the law but minimise unnecessary bureaucracy and waste of public resources. The Steering Group, chaired initially by Professor Kent Woods and subsequently by Professor Janet Darbyshire, involved the main stakeholders in UK publicly funded clinical trials, including funders, the Medicines and Healthcare Products Regulatory Agency (MHRA), university and Trust research managers, and academic trialists. One of the important achievements of the Project was to bring these groups together to work towards a shared objective. The results of this work and the advice developed by the six workstreams may be found in the Clinical Trials Toolkit (www.ct-toolkit.ac.uk).

Although much was achieved through the Joint Project a number of areas require further attention:

- coordination of approval processes before a trial begins
- the risk-averse behaviour of some institutions and investigators
- wider acceptance of a proportionate and risk-based approach to trial monitoring and pharmacovigilance proposed by the project
- sponsorship and insurance in international trials.

A survey of the impact the regulations on trials that were open when the new regulations were introduced and those due to start subsequently is currently being undertaken by the UK Clinical Trials Forum, UK Trial Managers Network and National Cancer Research Network (NCRN). Based on the initial responses for 61 ongoing and 31 new trials, many problems are being encountered, although there may be some reporting bias. The most common problem concerns sponsorship, reported for 40 (66%) of open and 18 (58%) of new trials and unresolved in 16 (26%) and 9 (29%). There was inevitably a knock-on effect on other aspects of a trial, including insurance and indemnity arrangements, host institution approvals, the addition of new trial sites and release of the medicinal product by a pharmaceutical company partner. Difficulties in identifying sponsors was the main reason for severe delays: five ongoing trials were suspended, four have been unable to add new sites and 10 of the new trials have been unable to start.

The establishment of the UKCRC, a partnership of the key organisations that influence research in the NHS, provides an important opportunity to ensure that regulatory and other administrative and bureaucratic hurdles do not prevent or delay clinical research in the UK. There is an urgent need to address the outstanding issues and inevitably new ones will arise. In addition, it will be essential to help researchers navigate the existing and forthcoming regulatory requirements with the overall aim of improving the regulatory environment and the quality of clinical research.

The future focus of public health research

Mike Kelly

The Health Development Agency (HDA) was established in 2000. It has the task, among others, of developing an evidence base for public health. Within that overall remit it has specifically focused on effectiveness, and especially the effectiveness of interventions that could reduce inequalities in health. Operationally this general aim was turned into three questions: What is effective? What is ineffective? And what is harmful or dangerous? When applying such principles to public health, there is a conundrum that has to be faced: while health at an aggregate level, for the population as a whole, has continued to improve year on year and decade on decade for the last 200 years, in the last 40 years or so, the inequalities gradient has steepened and the mortality differences between the most and least advantaged has widened. Things are getting better *and* worse simultaneously.

In order to begin the process of evidence building the HDA developed two products: Evidence Briefings and Evidence Reviews. *Evidence Briefings* are highly systematic tertiary level reviews of particular topics which identify the strengths and weaknesses of the evidence, gaps in the evidence, implications for policy and practice, and make recommendations for future research. *Evidence Reviews* are syntheses of the literature, summaries of key ideas or explorations of key concepts, theories or methods. Taken together these two series provide a unique resource which is a comprehensive, systematic and up-to-date map of the evidence. They may all be viewed at www.hda-online.org.uk/evidence.

Evidence Briefings have now been completed on the prevention of: teenage pregnancy, the transmission of HIV and STIs, the uptake of smoking, alcohol and drug misuse, accidental injury, low birth weight, suicide in young people and obesity and overweight. Briefings have also been published on the promotion of: smoking cessation, breast feeding, social support in pregnancy and physical activity. Evidence Reviews have been published on the prevention dividend in cancer and coronary heart disease, social capital, qualitative evidence, the life course and smoking-attributable deaths.

The review process has generated a number of findings that cut across the different topic areas but which provide a focus for the future direction of public health. Tailored and targeted interventions for particular population groups work best. Multilevel and multifaceted interventions and approaches also have a better track record of effectiveness. Approaches which are theoretically well informed report better results. If approaches or interventions involve information transmission, if it is clear and unambiguous it seems to work better and where services are integrated at local level and reflect community needs, they tend to do better too.

However, there are a number of problems with the existing state of the evidence which have emerged in the course of the review work. First, notwithstanding a rich literature describing the inequalities in health, the evidence for the effectiveness of interventions is small, especially with respect to reducing health inequalities. The HDA estimates that less than 0.5% of published papers by British researchers in public health and related disciplines actually dealt with intervention research as such. There is also a real paucity of cost-effectiveness data or, indeed, data to allow calculations of cost-effectiveness to be done.

Second, such as it is, there is more evidence about downstream interventions rather than upstream interventions. In other words there is an emphasis in the literature on things like individually-based interventions for promoting physical activity, rather than about the environmental factors such as traffic and parks which might promote physical activity.

Third, the theoretical and empirical descriptions of the population to map its social variations are underdeveloped. This is of vital importance because social variations are important mediating factors in the ways that different segments of the population respond to interventions. Categories for collecting data about the population and its description are still primarily organised around census occupational categories; and important as these are for providing aggregate accounts of mortality at population level, the fine-grained detail of the variegations in the population, and the importance of cultural and social differences, as well as the impact these have, is not well documented.

Fourth, the effectiveness literature is dominated by the randomised controlled trial (RCT). This is not a problem at one level because of course it is the right type of study design for determining effectiveness. However, it creates a 'knock-on' effect with respect to the hierarchy of evidence. In other words, because the RCT is so good at what it does, when done properly, some commentators see evidence derived from other sources as inferior. It also means that because of the way the research questions are set in RCTs, especially ones relating to process or to potential mediating factors (which are deliberately controlled out of most RCTs), they remain unanswered or undescribed.

Fifth, great care has to taken when working at tertiary review level, so that errors are not compounded. Because the HDA's Evidence Briefings are reviews of reviews, it is important to ensure that errors in original studies are not repeated through the systematic review process.

Finally, the HDA has had to think in detail about the problems of synthesising evidence from different research traditions. This is difficult and the HDA has not yet put in place a programme of work to take it forward. As always with evidence, the critical appraisal process used in compiling its base has to focus on the question of thresholds of quality, or of grading the evidence. Not all evidence is of uniformly good quality, so the ways of discriminating between different quality in evidence have been a preoccupation in much of the process itself. This has been done in the context of the quality of systematic reviews as well as the quality of primary studies.

The HDA has also considered a number of issues related to getting the evidence, once assembled, into practice. This is important because even the best quality scientific evidence does not say much about a number of very important factors that are highly significant in terms of making interventions work. Most reported studies report very little about how to do the intervention, at least as far as specific details of what took place interpersonally, organisationally or politically. Process data about the ins and outs of implementing the intervention are also very limited. The way that local infrastructures and local professionals engage with the process is significantly underreported. What the intervention consisted of is frequently not adequately described and because of the imperative in modern science towards generalisability, those factors borne out of specifically local factors are precisely those which are controlled out of experimental designs.

Local infrastructures, including such things as the degree of involvement of professional groups, the impact of local organisational arrangements, the impact of local politics and leadership, all play critical roles in the success or otherwise of an intervention. This has led the HDA to draw a distinction between knowledge to be derived directly from scientific studies (which provides a framework of plausible accounts of why things work) and knowledge derived from practice (which helps understand the likelihood of success of an intervention). Scientific plausibility may be made the more certain according to the degree to which the evidence may be regarded as strong. And of course there is a wide variety of tools to enable the Agency to grade evidence according to methodological rigour, and especially its internal validity. However, it does not follow that strong or good evidence produces strong recommendations for action. Guidance and recommendations can only be made after an assessment has been made of the mediating factors operating on the ground and embedded in local practice.

This assessment of the mediating factors is the type of knowledge which is concerned with the likelihood of success. What the HDA has done is to devise a method to derive this information. It involves simple collection of qualitative data from practitioners and attempting to get inside the meanings and understandings of local conditions as they interact with interventions. So the evidence is seen as a framework of plausible possibilities, and as a starting point for interventions, rather than as a recipe or imperative for action.

References

1   Kelly MP, Swann C, Morgan A, Killoran A, Naidoo B and Barnett-Paige E (2002)

Methodological Problems in Constructing the Evidence base in Public Health. Health Development Agency: London. www.hda-online.org.uk/evidence/meth_problems.html

2   Kelly MP (2004) *The evidence of effectiveness of public health interventions – and the implications.* Health Development Agency: London. www.hda-online.org.uk/documents/evidence_effective_briefing_paper.pdf

3   Kelly MP and Capewell S (2004) *Relative contributions of changes in risk factors and treatment to the reduction of coronary heart disease mortality.* Health Development Agency: London. www.hda-online.org.uk/Documents/cancer_under75s_briefing.pdf

4   Kelly MP, Chambers J, Huntley J and Millward L (2004) *Method 1 for the production of Effective Action Briefings and related materials.* Health Development Agency: London. www.hda-online.org.uk/evidence/EIP_Protocol_jan04_V4.pdf

5   Kelly MP, Crombie H and Owen L (2004) *The contribution of smoking, diet, screening and treatment to cancer mortality in the under 75s.* Health Development Agency: London. www.hda-online.org.uk/Documents/CHD_Briefing_nov_04.pdf

6   Kelly MP, Speller V and Meyrick J (2004) *Getting evidence into practice in public health.* Health Development Agency: London. www.hda-online.org.uk/documents/getting_eip_pubhealth.pdf

7   Kelly MP and Swann C (2004) Evidence into practice and health inequalities. *Health Education* **104**: 269–71.

8   Killoran A and Kelly MP (2004) Towards an evidence-based approach to tackling health inequalities: the English experience. *Health Education Journal* **63**: 7–14.

9   Graham H and Kelly MP (2004) Health inequalities: concepts, frameworks and policy. Health Development Agency: London. www.194.83.94.67/uhtbin/cgisirsi.exe/1100853936/0/520/Health_Inequalities_policy

10 Millward L, Kelly MP and Nutbeam D (2003) *Public Health Interventions Research: The Evidence.* Health Development Agency: London. www.hda-online.org.uk/evidence

11 Swann S, Falce C, Morgan A, Kelly M and Powell G (2003) *HDA Evidence base: Process and Quality Standards Manual for Evidence Briefings.* Health Development Agency: London. www.hda-online.org.uk/evidence/ebmanual_pqs.html

Putting clinical research into practice

Kirstine Knox and David J Kerr

Cancer – the challenge

Cancer is the second most common cause of death in the Western world. It is currently estimated that 1 in 3 women and 1 in 2 men living in developed countries will develop cancer at some point during their lifetime. The reasons for this are multifactorial and include environmental and lifestyle changes, together with advances in other areas of medicine. This means that the average lifespan of people in the West is increasing, and therefore so is the risk of developing cancer. It is almost certain that everyone in the West today who enjoys a normal lifespan, will be affected directly or indirectly by cancer at some time in their lives. The human and economic burdens of cancer to societies and governments are and will continue to be enormous unless we change these statistics.

Cancer is an abnormality in the genetic regulation and control of cellular growth and differentiation that results in profound changes in cellular behaviour. It can and does occur in every tissue of the body, resulting in some 110 different kinds of human malignancy. Therefore cancer is not one disease – even within a given histology – and is not derived from a single abnormal mechanism. This means that the current 'one size fits all' approach to therapeutic intervention, which has been successful in some cases, has likely reached its maximum potential clinical application and benefit. We need better approaches to therapeutic development.

Cancer – the opportunity

If we are to positively impact on cancer, we need to afford our researchers the environment in which they can harness the benefits of the molecular revolution in medicine, and development of modern informatics, by translating molecular research into innovative approaches to cancer. It is now widely accepted that as the introduction of cell culture techniques into biochemical laboratories in the 1960s enormously expanded our capacity to dissect complex, interacting metabolic and signal transduction pathways, so too will the application of gene sequencing, proteomic and polymerase chain reaction (PCR) methodologies to surgically harvested cancer and adjacent normal tissue. The concept of molecular signatures whereby the neoplastic tissue might be typed according to the pattern of gene and protein expression and correlated with cancer stage, prognosis and natural history is an important step towards individualising subsequent treatment selection. For example, whether adjuvant chemotherapy, radiotherapy or a mechanistically novel anti-cancer agent might prove appropriate. There is worldwide acceptance that such molecular profiling, facilitating the targeting and customisation of treatments, represents the next leap forward in improving the quality of care of cancer patients.

The answer – translational research and the translational research 'team'

The term 'translational research' is being increasingly used, yet there is no real consensus as to its meaning. One of the best definitions of translational research and of the translational research team comes from Dr Dennis Slamon at UCLA, who has been instrumental in the development of the revolutionary anti-cancer drug Herceptin® (trastuzmab). Dr Slamon defines translational research as 'the development and clinical application of basic science concept/discoveries and/or the investigation of important clinical questions in the laboratory with subsequent application back to the clinic'. This definition covers basic research in the laboratory together with research in the clinic involving patients, i.e. early phase and large randomised controlled trials. It means that the translational research team is the 'virtual' team which brings a new therapy from the laboratory to the patient and the clinic and comprises:

- basic research scientists and their support staff, who work to understand the molecular pathogenesis of cancer and identify potential targets for therapeutic intervention
- clinical researchers and their support staff, who work in the clinic with patients to test new therapies in clinical trials
- molecular pathologists and informaticians, who work to validate the potential of a new therapy using human tissue annotated with clinical information
- epidemiologists, statisticians and population biologists, who work, usually in association with large clinical trials involving hundreds if not thousands of patients, to understand whether new approaches offer benefits to patients
- industry – biotech and pharmaceutical – who likely cover the costs of some $800 million estimated to take a new drug from the laboratory to the clinic and the patient and
- patients, whose equal partnership in this process allows us to make progress in the treatment of cancer for the benefit of future generations.

Developing a solution for the UK

In the UK, the cancer research funders, who are known as the National Cancer Research Institute (NCRI), are supporting this model of translational research by:

- working through the NCRI partnership towards the provision of funding which supports the continua of the translational research process – from basic research to phase III trials – in a way which reflects the burden of disease at different sites of the body
- supporting the establishment of a new National Cancer Tissue Resource from 2005, developing a joint strategy for collection of tissue samples in the contest of clinical trials and developing a cancer informatics strategy and programme
- providing sustained critical core NHS infrastructure and workforce capability through National Translational Cancer Research Network (NTRAC) and NCRN. NTRAC is seeking to increase the national capacity and quality for the conduct of early phase cancer trials of therapeutic, diagnostic and preventative strategies. By collaborating with its sister organisation, the NCRN, which is charged with providing the NHS infrastructure and workforce to support large randomised phase III trials, NTRAC is providing a strong scientific support and evidence base for therapeutic development and cancer care pathways. The sustained funding for critical core NHS infrastructure and workforce is provided through NTRAC and particularly through NCRN, which increased patient accrual from 3.4% to 10.8% into phase III trials in a little over two years. Improved clinical outcomes for patients will come from national guidance based on the best available evidence
- involving patients, patients representatives and the public in all aspects of their work
- working to involve industry.

The NCRI and the cancer research networks, have been a persuasive model for the DH's recent success in creating the UKCRC in April 2004 following recommendations made in interim and final reports of the Research for Patient Benefit Working Party. One of its core initiatives is to apply the model of the cancer research networks to other disease areas including mental health, children's medicine, diabetes, Alzheimer's disease and stroke. In 2004 the Government committed £100 million over the next four years to this project.

Why is translational research important?

It is only through the translation of today's science that we will benefit tomorrow's patient. Evidence of success is already demonstrable. For example, Dr Slamon's work, to develop the revolutionary anti-cancer drug Herceptin®

(trastuzmab), which results in increased survival of a defined subsection of breast cancer patients, is a success story that demonstrates the potential of modern, rational drug design and development. Briefly, groundbreaking observations made in 1987, in tumour samples from 189 breast cancer patients enrolled in an ongoing study demonstrated that the gene that codes for HER2 is amplified in 20–30% of human breast cancers. Two years later, examining the gene and its RNA and protein products in more than 650 frozen and paraffin-embedded human breast cancer samples, demonstrated that amplification of the HER2 gene correlates strongly with poor clinical progress. From here, partnership with Genetech resulted in the humanised, anti-HER2 antibody, Herceptin®. The clinical benefits of Herceptin® would almost certainly have been insufficient for Food and Drug Administration (FDA) approval if the agent had been tested in unselected patient populations. We know today that Herceptin® is saving women's lives.

Further information

Further information can be found at:

- NCRI: www.ncri.org.uk
- NCRI informatics initiative: www.cancerinformatics.org.uk
- NCRN: www.ncrn.org.uk
- NTRAC: www.ntract.org.uk

Effective ways for implementing research in a clinical environment: benefits, barriers and future challenges

Adrian Davis

There are huge benefits for patients and gains in effectiveness and efficiency for the NHS which can be made if the clinical implications of research are put into practice. Research can make a difference to the health of the nation and the future of the NHS if the barriers to implementation are broken down. Too often research is left unused, or left until it is too late or is implemented in an inappropriate context or without proper training, thus doing more harm than good! Translating what has worked in research into action is poorly understood. The culture of the Research Assessment Exercise (RAE), the Quality Assurance Agency (QAA) and clinical directors' priorities all mitigate against effective and appropriate implementation of the evidence base. There are very few incentives for researchers and clinicians to form partnerships that deliver better services. The challenge is to provide that partnership, to develop leadership and capacity in translational research and to break the 20-year cycle of 'research into practice'. To do this we need:

1   a research governance framework that enables rather than stifles efforts to put good research into practice and
2   an evaluative culture in service development and provision that enables widespread implementation that is effective throughout the NHS whilst being fine-tuned to meet local requirements within that national context.

Examples from my experience about providing capacity in the NHS using public–private sector partnerships and in working with the National Screening Committee to deliver newborn screening provide some good examples of how evaluative culture can be introduced to NHS services.

In particular we have researched new ways of working with the independent sector over the last year that have led to the formation of a framework contract for hearing aid services supply to the NHS that is being taken up by roughly half the hearing aid sites in England during 2004/05. Our conclusions were that:

- Private Public Partnership (PPP) has greatly enhanced the capacity of the NHS Hearing Aid Services to deliver modernised services to meet the needs of the hearing impaired. It was clear from earlier work (refereed report for DH) that equal, if not better, outcomes were obtained in using the PPP compared to NHS services. However it was concluded that ongoing evaluation and particularly quality assurance of the PPP was essential to delivering a safe, truly additive and cost-effective service. The initial pilot study looked at quality issues around plurality of provision at two participating site and this has been extended to an take account of seven sites that were subsequently commissioned.
- Focus groups showed that patients' experience of PPP is a positive one. All are grateful to have had their hearing aid/s fitted earlier than expected by a private hearing aid dispenser.
- All were happy with the professional and courteous manner in which they had been treated by the private dispensers. And when asked, over 95% of attendees at the focus groups were extremely satisfied with the service, giving it a score of 9 or 10/10.
- A few patients required adjustments to their aid/s between fitting and follow-up. In these instances, their experiences were less satisfactory. These patients felt as if the dispenser was reluctant to deal with their problem. This may be an indication that dispensers are disinclined to deal with situations that fall outside of the agreed contract. This has been changed in the framework contract.
- NHS audiologists initially regarded PPP with some suspicion but most now see it as a necessary addition to the Modernising Hearing Aid Services (MHAS) process.
- Lack of suitable software and appropriate computer hardware is the biggest stumbling block for the effective implementation of PPP protocols. It seems absurd that sites participating in the scheme were not equipped from the outset with the means to collect, monitor and analyse their data properly.
- Quality assurance of the PPP framework programme needs to be active at the local and national level in order to ensure good quality patient experience and value for money.

The research, procurement and service development that have led to the PPP have been working closely together so that the procurement and service development are evidence-based and are delivered as quickly and safely as possible. This is possible partly because of the evaluative culture that we have promoted in modernisation at all hearing aid centres (168 in England) and the introduction of appropriate IT. The residual difficulty is in making that IT securely available to the private sector. There appears to be a general need to be able to develop translational research capacity to run this sort of research and development in coordination so that the research is translated into action and patients benefiting from the research within a year or so, rather than the usual 20-year cycle! The major advantage gained from PPP was compliance with national patient journeys and guidelines.

Research ethics: a barrier or gateway to quality research?

Simon Woods

Everyone reading this piece will recognise the importance of two key words, 'Nuremberg'[1] and 'Helsinki', in shaping the contemporary approach to research ethics. The Nuremberg Code was the first foundational international ethics framework for biomedical research and formed the basis of the Declaration of Helsinki.[2] However it was not until the 'Tokyo' version of Helsinki that the need for ethical review of research was stipulated and hence the close association between research quality and ethics was forged. However such a need had already been identified in the UK:

- 1967: Royal College of Physicians (RCP) recommends independent review of research proposals.
- 1967: Publication of Pappworth's *Human Guinea Pigs: Experiments on man.*[3]
- 1975: RCP's recommendations for independent review endorsed by DH – establishment of informal ethics committees followed.
- 1991: DH requires establishment of formal ethics committees and issues guidelines (*Health Service Guideline* **91**: 5).
- 2001: Research Governance Framework for Health and Social Care (DH)

Now every health authority in the UK has at least one Local Research Ethics Committee (LREC) and Multi-centre Research Ethics Committees (MRECs), which are regionally based, both providing ethical reviews of health research applications. With the introduction of the new Statutory Instrument (2004) governing the control of clinical trials we are now the closest we have ever been to establishing Research Ethics Committees on a statutory basis.

Before we become too self-congratulatory on the basis of this evidence of obvious moral progress we must acknowledge that the picture is slightly more complicated. Critics of the regulatory 'snowball' have observed a darker and possibly unethical dimension to research ethics regulation. These critics warn of a tragedy, not of the same *kind* as the Nazi atrocities, but possibly on a similar scale. The argument is that research ethics, construed as research regulation, rather than enhancing research quality is in fact detrimental to it.

Some evidence

From its earliest versions the Declaration of Helsinki sets out a number of moral 'home truths' that are so self-evident as to be beyond question. Research participants are vulnerable, and within this population some are more vulnerable than others. It goes almost without saying that children are amongst some of the most vulnerable research participants and therefore the precautionary measures taken when conducting research with children must be set proportionately high. The problem as some would see it is that too strict an interpretation of this injunction has been detrimental to children. There are certain conditions that affect only children, and there are treatments used for children that have not been properly researched for use in children. Children are disadvantaged by this position but placed in *double jeopardy* by the reluctance to allow children to participate in research. So children are worse off for the mere fact that they are children.

In the late 1970s a team of researchers designed a large placebo-controlled trial to investigate the possible association between spina bifida and vitamin deficiency. The research ethics committees reviewing the application raised an objection to having a placebo group on the basis that 'vitamins are good for you'. The trial went ahead and was published but was criticised for being scientifically flawed. After much acrimonious debate a new trial was set up which took eight years and £8 million to prove that the original trial had in fact found a real effect.[4]

The knock to public trust and confidence following the tissue retention scandals of Bristol and Alder Hey have had an impact not just on research affecting children but all medical research which involves human tissue. The result has been what some would see as another turn of the regulatory screw and the introduction of yet another tier of statute in the form of the proposed Human Tissue Bill and the establishment of the Human Tissue Authority.

The undermining of confidence is not solely confined to members of the public with evidence that health professionals are increasingly reluctant to engage in research and less willing to seek consent from patients for certain kinds of research.

Argawal *et al.*[5] report the effects of the introduction into surgical consent forms of a space for patients to indicate consent or objection to the subsequent use of any residual material for research or teaching. An audit showed that only 48% of specimens received in the laboratory had traceable consent forms, 40% of which did not have the 'tissue' section completed. Of the completed forms, only 0.8% objected to research use, but 8% objected to use in 'public health monitoring'. This apparent contradiction suggests serious deficiencies in the quality of information provided to patients by the surgeons. Other examples collated by the Wellcome Trust and submitted in evidence for the Human Tissue Bill included evidence that the decline in post-mortems in one Trust was due almost entirely to clinical staff failing to ask for consent from next of kin. In another example a breast cancer research unit was unable to obtain normal breast tissue controls because surgical colleagues felt they did not have time to explain the research use of residual tissue in order to obtain patient's consent. This reluctance reflects not only the fact that researchers feel burdened by a burgeoning bureaucracy but also lack the confidence to engage with a perceived critical public.

Bristol and Alder Hey were scandals because some of the medical profession had begun to take too much for granted. However, an irresponsible press and an emotive public response exacerbated the problem further.

The above discussion is an indicator of how the quality of research, indeed whether research is carried out at all is influenced by the bureaucracy of 'ethics' and regulation, a failure of the researchers and policers of research to see eye to eye, and a lack of public engagement and understanding with research.

The solution?

Medical research is in all our interests, since we all stand to benefit either directly or indirectly from healthcare that is efficacious and safe. So how should a society that values these benefits characterise the expectations it has of its citizens if they are to enjoy these benefits? One could talk of a moral duty such that all those who expect to benefit should be expected to reciprocate through cooperation with research. I prefer to put this in terms of a *moral* expectation that each person, the young, the old, the infirm and the healthy, will contribute to medical research. However, before we can begin to articulate this expectation a number of issues must be addressed. First, the public must be assured that their trust is not misplaced.[6] Therefore they must be assured of the quality of the research and the quality of the regulation of the research. They must also be informed and able to engage in the many debates that contemporary medical research stimulates. This means a commitment to providing education for our youngest citizens as well as for adults. The media should also acknowledge its contribution to the mêlée and be allowed to make this but through an informed and responsible approach.

Finally, there needs to be greater congruence between researchers and those who are the guardians of research ethics. Researchers must be trained to see that ethics is not an optional extra just as members of RECs, advisory bodies and regulators must have a more professional insight into the research process.

So more and better ethics, leading to more and better research requires informed and reflective professionals and public.

References

1   The Nuremberg Code (1947) In: A Mitscherlich and F Mielke (1949) *Doctors of infamy: the story of the Nazi medical crimes.* Schuman: New York. xxiii-xxv [published online at: www.cirp.org/library/ethics/nuremberg/].

2   World Medical Association Declaration of Helsinki (2004) *Ethical principles for medical research involving human subjects*. WMA: Tokyo.

3   Pappworth MH (1967) *Human Guinea Pigs: Experiments on man*. Routledge Kegan Paul: London.

4   Personal communication from Professor John Burn University of Newcastle.

5   Agarwal, Sugden and Quirke (2003) Introduction of consent for surgically removed tissue. *J Pathol* **201**(Supp.): 49A.

6   O'Neill O (2002) *Autonomy and Trust in Bioethics*. Cambridge University Press: Cambridge.

PART TWO

Striving for excellence

Looking backwards to the future

Michael D Rawlins

NICE – the National Institute for Clinical Excellence – was set up five and a half years ago[1] with a remit to 'provide health professionals in England and Wales with advice on securing the highest attainable standards of care for National Health Service patients'. The Institute does this through three programmes: technology appraisals, clinical guidelines and interventional procedures.[2]

Appraisals of health technologies, and the development of clinical guidelines for the management of individual conditions, are based on considerations of both clinical and cost-effectiveness. The interventional procedures programme is concerned solely with safety and efficacy; although those that fulfil certain criteria may subsequently go forward for a full appraisal.

Over the five years of its existence the Institute has completed, and published, more than 200 individual forms of NICE guidance (*see* Figure A). These include 89 appraisals (involving over 250 individual products), 32 clinical guidelines (ranging from antenatal care to palliative care) and 95 interventional procedures. And there is more to come: during the next three years NICE expects to publish the results of over 50 technology appraisals, 44 clinical guidelines, and (at the current rate of notifications) advice on the safety and efficacy of at least 100 new interventional procedures.

In the beginning, though, things were not easy. One of our most trenchant critics was Richard Smith – the editor of the *British Medical Journal*. He gave us a lukewarm welcome, in 1999, with an editorial headlined 'NICE: a panacea for the NHS?'[3] A year later[4] he had given up on the Institute with an editorial headed 'The failings of NICE' and the claim that it was time to start on version 2. It was, therefore, extraordinary to read in the *British Medical Journal* – in 2004 – Richard Smith's headline 'The Triumph of NICE'.[5] And when he wrote, in the first paragraph, 'NICE may prove to be one of Britain's greatest cultural exports along with Shakespeare, Milton, the Beatles, Harry Potter and the Teletubbies', amazement gave way to incredulity. But he finished the piece, in more sombre (and characteristic) vein, with a 'could do better' remark. This is a sentiment with which I concur.

The green shoots of the acceptance of NICE, by the editor of the *British Medical Journal*, are reflected in the views of the public. An opinion poll, carried

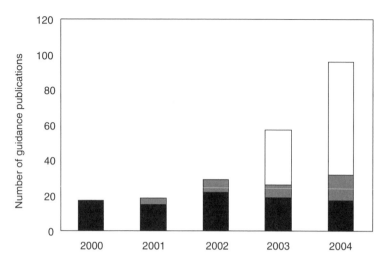

Figure A   Annual numbers of individual forms of NICE guidance as technology appraisals (black), clinical guidelines (grey) and interventional procedures (white).

out in March this year indicated that 27% of the public was aware of NICE and that 72% of those who had heard of NICE viewed us 'quite positively' or 'very positively'. And interest in, and knowledge about, NICE comes not only from Britain but from overseas. In November 2004 we had a record number (almost 4 million) of hits on our website. Half of these were from the UK; and the rest from overseas – with the US being our most frequent overseas visitor. So what has happened, over these past five and a half years, for the Institute to have gained acceptance by even its fiercest critics?

The basis of NICE guidance

NICE guidance is based on fundamental principles.[6]

1   NICE guidance is clinically and technically robust and is based on a full, systematic review of the relevant literature. Moreover, the modelling techniques used in the economic analyses meet high standards. The quality of NICE guidance is the Institute's most precious asset.
2   NICE is as transparent in its processes, and the evidence at its disposal, as is humanly possible. And the Institute tries to be equally as open about both its interpretation of the evidence, and the reasons why its advisory bodies have reached their conclusions.
3   NICE involves all relevant stakeholders. These include relevant professional bodies, industries, patient and carer organisations, and (especially in the

guidelines programme) service users themselves. And whilst they do not always get their 'way', they can always have their 'say'.

4   NICE guidance is constructed by independent members of our advisory bodies drawn from the NHS and academia. Whilst the Institute's board has, as it must, reserve powers to overrule an advisory body's conclusions, it has never yet done so.

5   NICE guidance is not the creation of the Institute's board or its staff. NICE is a virtual institute involving several thousand people across the UK. The appraisal committees depend, heavily, on the Technology Assessment Groups based in universities stretching from Aberdeen to the West Country. The National Collaborating Centres (NCCs), largely formed around the Royal Medical, Nursing and Midwifery Colleges, develop the Institute's guidelines with their independent guideline development groups and review groups. And the Interventional Procedures Advisory Committee is supported by several hundred specialist advisors from the NHS as well as a Review Body based on a consortium of universities.

NICE is also dependent on its stakeholders and consultees from industry, a wide range of professional bodies, and an even broader span of patient–carer organisations. They all help ensure that NICE guidance is contextually appropriate; they are all crucial components of the 'virtual' institute that is essential to the work and credibility of NICE.

The future

Richard Smith was correct when he claimed[5] that NICE 'Could do better'.

1   There are various aspects of the Institute's methodologies and processes that need overhauling. In particular, the way topics are selected is still not ideal. They are ultimately agreed by health ministers but the list of potential topics is drawn up, jointly, by officials from the DH and the Institute. But it is too 'top down'. The Department and NICE need to gather proposals from NHS staff, as well as patients and their carers, about the guidance topics they would like the Institute to prepare. A web-based topic selection proposal scheme has therefore been placed on the NICE website.

2   When NICE was set up the implementation of its guidance was excluded from its terms of reference. In retrospect this was a mistake and one for which I must take some responsibility. For I have always maintained[1] that unless its guidance is implemented, and makes a difference to people, it is a waste of time and money.

Several studies on the implementation of NICE guidance have now been undertaken. Probably the most comprehensive, and relevant, is that by Abacus International[7] examining the extent to which 28 individual forms of NICE guidance have been adopted in the NHS. The results show that in four instances there has been 'over-implementation' (whereby the uptake of technologies has, rightly or wrongly, been substantially greater than antici- pated); 12 pieces of guidance have been 'fully implemented'; and 12 have been 'under-implemented'. This is not a disaster – NICE is clearly having a substantial effect – but it is not good enough. More needs to be done.

It is important to recognise that the issue of how to ensure that the results of research get into clinical practice is not a uniquely British problem. For NICE, though, there are four key issues to address:

- Does the right person get the guidance? And is it in the right form at the time it is needed?
- Does this 'right' person want to do anything with it? If not, why not?
- Can anything more be done to help with implementation even if there is commitment? Or are there financial or organisational impediments standing in the way?
- Finally, has implementation been successful?

Through NICE's newly established Implementation Systems programme the Institute intends to do everything possible to improve the implementation of its guidance including helping forward planning, providing implementation toolkits and ensuring access to simple audit methods.

3 The most significant challenge NICE faces, from 1 April 2005, is to provide guidance that will inform the practice of public health. This, until now, has been the responsibility of the HDA but its functions, budget and staff are to transfer to the Institute.[8]

From 2005 NICE will become responsible for helping to improve the health of the population as well as that of individual patients. It will be expected to produce guidance that maintains health as well as meets the needs of those who are unwell, and it will involve developing guidance to support the main elements of health promotion. These additional responsibil- ities offer a real opportunity for NICE to make a difference to people's lives in three ways.

- First, it will allow the Institute to incorporate an economic component into the valuable, and highly original, work already started by the HDA. Like clinical practice, there is an imperative in public health to use the nation's resources in a manner that will yield the greatest benefits for us all. NICE will adapt the expertise it has gained over the past few years to bring this to fruition.
- Second, it will allow NICE to contribute to the ambitious programme laid out in the recent public health white paper.
- Third, and possibly most important of all, it will encourage the Institute to incorporate public health messages and strategies across its clinical guidance programmes. Over the last few decades, in Britain as in other countries, something of a 'silo' mentality has grown up between clini- cians and public health specialists. Clinicians, especially those in primary

care, already make significant contributions to public health. So, but to a lesser extent, do clinicians who work in the secondary and tertiary sectors. But all could, and should, do more. Over the next five years of its existence NICE will make it happen.

Conclusion

There is, in some respects, a new start for NICE – a 'New NICE' – which will continue to provide guidance to front-line NHS health professionals but will also incorporate the interests of the wider public health community. It will be both the same – and different.

References

1   Rawlins MD (1999) In pursuit of quality: the National Institute for Clinical Excellence. *The Lancet* **353**: 1079–82.

2   National Institute for Clinical Excellence (2004) *A Guide to NICE*. National Institute for Clinical Excellence: London. www.nice.org.uk

3   Smith R (1999) NICE: a panacea for the NHS? *BMJ* **318**: 823–4.

4   Smith R (2000) The failings of NICE. *BMJ* **321**: 1363–4.

5   Smith R (2004) The triumph of NICE. *BMJ* **329**: 234.

6   Rawlins MD (2004) NICE work – providing guidance to the British National Health Service. *New England Journal of Medicine* **351**: 1383–6.

7   Abacus International (2004) *Implementing NICE guidance*. National Institute for Clinical Excellence: London. www.nice.org.uk

8   Department of Health (2004) *Reconfiguring the Department of Health's Arm's Length Bodies*. Department of Health: London.

Measuring what matters: a new approach to assessment

Anna Walker

The NICE Conference, and the launch of the Healthcare Commission's consultation on our new approach to performance assessment, presents a good opportunity to look at the implementation of NICE guidance in healthcare organisations.

About the Healthcare Commission

The Healthcare Commission's fundamental purpose is to promote improvement in health and healthcare in England. Our main statutory duties are to:

- assess the management, provision and quality of NHS healthcare (including, for the first time, public health)
- review the performance of each NHS trust and award an annual performance rating
- publish information about the state of healthcare
- consider complaints about NHS organisations that the organisations themselves have not resolved
- promote the coordination of reviews and assessments carried out by others
- regulate the independent healthcare sector through registration, annual inspection and enforcement
- carry out investigations of serious failures in the provision of healthcare.

Assessment for improvement: principles for a new approach

On 29 November 2004, we published our consultation document, *Assessment for improvement – Our approach*, outlining our proposals for a new approach to performance assessment of organisations providing healthcare in the NHS and independent sectors in England.

The current system of assessment (or star ratings) will continue until 2006. This system concentrates on performance against the Government's targets for NHS organisations. We will continue to assess against these existing targets, but hope that our proposed new approach will provide a richer picture of how an organisation is performing.

We want to publish assessments that are relevant to patients, the public, healthcare managers and clinicians, and that are really measuring what matters. Our consultation will help us identify what is important for each of our audiences, so that we can provide useful and robust information. While our approach will be broader, the Commission is determined that it should make assessment less of a burden for those inspected. Our new approach will not involve large teams of inspectors routinely visiting organisations, and will not require a large bespoke collection of data as a matter of routine.

We will build on an organisation's own resources and make better use of the information readily available to us, such as other regulators' assessments, to target our interventions where there is cause for concern. Our interventions will be robust where standards are slipping, but when organisations have demonstrated good performance and effective leadership, our assessments will have a 'lighter touch'.

What will we be assessing?

Organisations will be assessed against a number of different measures including the Government's standards (common to all healthcare organisations) as well as existing and new targets. The standards cover a much wider range of an organisation's activities including safety, clinical effectiveness, patient focus and public health. In 2005/06, we intend to concentrate on assessing the compliance of NHS organisations against core standards. But, as public confidence grows that these standards are being met, we will focus more and more on assessments of developmental standards that promote continuous improvement.

The assessments we make of the performance of NHS trusts are designed to help answer two questions:

1   Is the organisation getting the basics right?
2   Is it making and sustaining progress?

Figure A illustrates the framework for our assessments. The trust's annual performance rating will be made up of a number of components, assessed and reported on individually.

For 2005/06, we will concentrate on whether organisations are 'getting the basics right' and to what degree they are meeting the core standards. We will:

● require Trust boards to make public declarations on the extent to which their organisation meets these core standards. Trusts will have to include

Framework of Assessment		
Compliance with core standards	Getting the basics right	Annual review and rating
Existing targets		
Use of resources		
Other regulatory findings		
Progress in meeting developmental standards	Making and sustaining progress	
New national targets		
Local targets		

Figure A Framework of assessment.

the views of patients, and other partners in the local health economy, in their declaration (patient forums, local authorities and strategic health authorities). We will check these declarations against other available information and follow up where there are concerns
- assess Trusts' performance in meeting the existing targets that all NHS organisations are expected to meet in 2003–06
- review Trusts' use of resources and the value for money that they provide. We will base this assessment on the work done by the Audit Commission and Monitor, so we are not creating new burdens
- use other findings from the Healthcare Commission, other regulators and recognised independent reviewers, as part of the assessment.

From 2005/06, we will also develop our proposals for assessing improvement with reference to the developmental standards. These point to the improvements that the Government expects all NHS Trusts to make. We will:

- assess the performance of NHS Trusts in working towards new national priorities and targets for improved outcomes and better experiences of healthcare for patients
- over time, assess the performance of NHS Trusts working towards local targets
- carry out improvement reviews, which will assess the quality of healthcare by reference to developmental standards and the patient's experience across and between healthcare organisations

Assessing the implementation of NICE guidance

NICE guidance is a key component of the national standards to which the NHS will be expected to work. Technology appraisals and interventional procedure reviews are reflected in the core standards, while clinical guidelines are regarded as developmental standards (Table A).

Table A Core and developmental standards

Core standards	
C3	Healthcare organisations protect patients by following NICE interventional procedures guidance
C5a)	Healthcare organisations ensure that they conform to NICE technology appraisals and, where it is available, take into account nationally agreed guidance when planning and delivering treatment and care

Developmental standard	
D2	Patients receive effective treatment and care that conforms to nationally agreed best practice, particularly as defined in national service frameworks, NICE guidance, national plans and agreed national guidance on service delivery

The inclusion of NICE guidance in these standards is a clear signal of its significance. Inclusion in assessments should encourage the NHS to ensure that implementation processes are in place, and spread best practice, in line with our duty to promote improvement. Our assessments should also be able to identify some of the problems or constraints on implementing guidance.

Our consultation outlines some of the prompts we will use to establish whether an organisation is meeting the core standards. We want to know whether we have got this right by listening to the views of others. We are also in the process of establishing a clinical effectiveness reference group of experts and patients, in order to define a process around the developmental standards, including compliance with NICE clinical guidelines.

In addition, our improvement reviews, which might focus on a particular condition or patient group, will take account of relevant NICE guidance. Three improvement reviews that are currently under way already do so: coronary heart disease, mental health and older people's services.

Moving forward

Over the past few months we have been working in partnership with a number of organisations and groups to develop our new approach to assessment. While we are clear about the principles, we are serious about consulting on the details and, in particular, on the specific prompts in relation to the core standards.

The consultation is on our website (www.healthcarecommission.org.uk). We are keen to hear from anyone interested in or involved with healthcare in order to develop an approach which is meaningful to all those who deliver or use healthcare.

If you would like hard copies of our consultation document or further information please contact our help desk on +44 (0)845 601 3012.

PART THREE

Commissioning for quality in mental health

Commissioning mental health services

Alan Cohen

Commissioning mental health services is integral to developing and providing mental health services. Historically the principle has been applied to the purchasing or procuring of services: the services purchased by the Health Authority or the primary care trust (PCT), and provided by a specialist mental health trust. More recently commissioning has been distinguished from purchasing, as the process of service redesign encompassing opinion and support from both purchaser and provider, so that a true partnership is developed between those who assess patient need and those who provide the care for a specific population. It has been likened to the difference between buying half a dozen eggs, and designing the supermarket from which the eggs are bought. With the publication of the National Service Framework (NSF) for Mental Health in 1999, and the development of performance targets based on the NSF, and the even more detailed Policy Implementation Guides for each of the elements of specialist services, commissioning took on a slightly different role. There was no flexibility with commissioner or provider as to what type of service could be commissioned. To extend the simile – it is as though a ready-designed supermarket is being put in place that will work in every location in the country. The role of a mental health commissioner in such a situation is one of organisational development – facilitating the development of a pre-designed service model, rather than trying to develop a locally specific model of care.

Throughout the above description of the meaning of 'commissioning' there was the presumption that the PCT was commissioning a service from a specialist provider. However, with the advent of the new General Medical Services (GMS) contract in April 2004, and the even more recent *Guidance on Practice Based Commissioning* in October 2004, there is a real opportunity to commission a service from primary care providers. Since the NSF does not make any specification of what primary care mental health services should or might look like there is a real opportunity to develop a locally sensitive service.

The effect of people with mental health problems in primary care is not insignificant, in relation to the disability that it creates, as well as in the impact of sheer numbers and costs associated with providing care to such a large number of people:

- 3 in 10 working age people have sick leave in any one year due to mental illness
- 91 million lost working days
- about 1 million people have been on long-term sick leave due to mental illness and receiving incapacity benefit (IB)
- < 10% are in contact with specialist mental health services

the proportion returning to employment, after having been on IB for 12 months or more is less than 5%.

And also on primary care services:

- some 30% of general practice consultations have a significant mental health component
- 90% of all people with a mental health disorder are managed entirely in primary care
- it is estimated that the costs of this care is £898m
- the cost of psychotropic drugs prescribed by primary care are calculated to be a further £754m
- 50% of sequential attenders at acute hospital outpatients have unexplained physical symptoms.

To develop a service that addresses the needs of such a large and disparate group is clearly of importance, and the recent developments since April 2004 makes that commissioning much easier.

nGMS

The new GMS contract for general practitioners (GPs) set out for the first time three levels of care: essential services that GPs had to provide, a set of additional services that they could choose to provide, and finally the opportunity for PCTs to commission an enhanced service, above and beyond that provided in essential services from either GPs or other providers. Enhanced services can be 'directed' – have to be commissioned by the PCT, nationally agreed minimum specification for a service, and finally a local service, that is really up to the PCT to decide.

Whilst the three levels of services form one part of remuneration to GPs, there is an extra contractual development called the Quality and Outcome Framework (QOF) that awards points to practices for achieving particular outcomes. There are in total 1050 points available to each practice, each point worth £75 in 2004–2005. Of those 1050 points, 550 represent positive outcomes in clinical domains, e.g. coronary heart disease, diabetes, including one clinical domain on mental illness. Within each clinical domain are a number of steps towards achieving full points and the best possible outcome for patients.

For mental health the five steps and associated points are shown in Table A.

Table A The Quality and Outcome Framework: Mental Health Indicator

Indicator	Points
Records	
MH 1. The practice can produce a register of people with severe long-term mental health problems who require and have agreed to regular follow-up	7
Ongoing management	
MH 2. The percentage of patients with severe long-term mental health problems with a review recorded in the preceding 15 months. This review includes a check on the accuracy of prescribed medication, a review of physical health and a review of co-ordination arrangements with secondary care	23
MH 3. The percentage of patients on lithium therapy with a record of lithium levels checked within the previous 6 months	3
MH 4. The percentage of patients on lithium therapy with a record of serum creatinine and TSH in the preceding 15 months	3
MH 5. The percentage of patients on lithium therapy with a record of lithium levels in the therapeutic range within the previous 6 months	5

Whilst there has been some interesting debate as to whether these targets of positive outcome within the mental health domain are appropriate, they are nevertheless what has been nationally negotiated and approved.

However, the overall negotiation process of the new GMS contract acknowledged that PMS (personal medical services) practices, which represent nearly 50% of all practices in the UK, were in part excluded. As a way of bringing the two contracts closer together, PMS practices also became eligible for payments associated with the QOF, as well as having the opportunity to create their own clinical domains.

The NICE guidelines for anxiety have used this flexibility to create a clinical domain for anxiety disorders. The process for developing a guideline is clearly set down, and involves at least two draft sets of guidelines which are commented on and reviewed by anybody who has nominated themselves as a stakeholder. Despite many comments about the recommendations in the guidance, there were no comments at all about a draft QOF for Generalised Anxiety Disorder, since it was buried in the audit section.

The new GMS contract allows commissioners to develop locally sensitive 'enhanced' services, that fit local needs. The criteria for developing such a service are that they need to be based on best practice and best available evidence. The development of national guidelines in a specific area of care such as depression provides the evidence base from which a locally enhanced service can be created.

The depression guideline talks about a stepped care approach to managing depression. There is an intermediate step that is proposed between standard primary and standard secondary care services. It could be considered an enhanced level of primary care, and indeed it is possible to develop an enhanced specification of care based entirely on the sort of care that could be provided at this level. The Sainsbury Centre for Mental Health is trying to develop such a level of care by working with five PCTs around the country. More details of the progress over the last 12 months is available on the Sainsbury Centre website www.scmh.org.uk.

In October 2004, the DH published guidance on practice-led commissioning. Although there may be concerns about individual practices commissioning specialist mental health services, there is a real opportunity for practices to commission effective interventions for conditions such as somatisation disorder. The attraction of this approach is that it provides a psychological intervention for people who have multiple physical complaints but no explained underlying physical illness. It further provides a funding route for a new service – by reducing outpatient attendance of people with somatisation disorder, the savings are used to employ specialists who can provide the effective psychological interventions. Identifying effective interventions are provided by the NICE guideline process.

In conclusion, there are a number of opportunities for PCTs to commission primary care mental health services, using the flexibilities within the new GMS contract, and using the NICE guidelines as the evidence base for ensuring that services are both effective and high quality.

Commissioning quality in mental health

Janet Millar

It was that bald statement in the NSF for Mental Health, so long ago, that threw down the gauntlet to primary care.

Any service user who contacts their primary care team with a common mental health problem should be identified and assessed and offered effective treatment including referral. The NSF was demanding the best in primary mental healthcare.

And, of course, it makes sense. We know that it is within primary care that we deal with the bulk of the mental distress, mild, moderate and severe, in the population – or fail adequately to deal with it! Therein lies the dilemma. Nevertheless, all of us working in primary care wish and strive to provide the best care for our patients with mental health problems.

In primary care we watch the unfolding of family dynamics and the source of much mental distress. We watch the child present with abdominal pain of anxiety and powerlessness. Our needy adolescent patients are still our patients as young adults and are not lost in that strange vacuum between secondary care services based on age. We listen to the struggles of the carer, and we see the impact of individual mental health problems spread through families, schools, workplaces and neighbourhoods. We hold the potential to deliver an innovative, exciting and effective mental health service.

Many of us have tried to change the mental health services. Many of us have become frustrated in the process of change. I have sat on very many committees over the years, in the vain understanding that I was helping to commission. Secondary care mental health services, for historical and financial reasons, are not sufficiently vulnerable to the commissioning process.

There is a push for primary care to consider practice-based commissioning and take on indicative commissioning budgets to contract services from secondary care. We can feel the momentum from the PCTs. The PCTs are feeling the push from on high.

But should we commission? Who should commission? And what should we commission?

There has to be gain in quality from the commissioning change. We have got a lot on our plates in primary care at the moment; do we really want to take on the intricate process of commissioning a complicated service from secondary care? Could we make it better for our patients? The lack of national tariffs and the danger of fragmentation of the secondary service should make us think twice. I cannot clearly see a way of influencing patient experience within secondary care from the small powerbase of the practice.

A major problem is that there is not a clear way to raise money to commission secondary services. There is the possibility of clawing back some money from psychiatric outpatients, but that might result in a loss of the goodwill services. Locally, our secondary care provider has supported us with link workers and practice-based anxiety management cognitive behaviour therapy (CBT). It holds hands with us. Sometimes the grasp is slippery, sometimes warm and firm. The commissioning process needs to reflect that complex system.

That could change, but the small unit of practice-based commissioning will not be sufficiently influential to take it on just yet. At the moment it seems that the PCT is the smallest unit to effectively negotiate for the secondary care services.

However, we could draw a different boundary between what has been considered secondary care and primary care and how we commission for both. Much of what we successfully hold and manage in general practice is serious mental illness. With an increased confidence and skill mix in the primary care team, we could effectively treat much more without referral. The referral gap to secondary care in terms of time, geography and significance can seem enormous to the patient.

We need to focus on commissioning a range of services for primary care. The requirement will be based on widening the opportunities for referral. Many practices already have good triage, counselling provision for all, cognitive behavioural therapy if appropriate, link workers from secondary care in every practice, easy and timely access to a broad range of psychological therapies, good use and connections with the non-statutory services, self-help and support groups. But patients still slither through the primary care experience without adequate assessment or therapeutic contact.

There are difficulties with any commissioning at practice level: management burden, more opportunities to wake sweating in the night, lack of practice space, potential loss of peer support and supervision structure for the mental health workers, loss of PCT clout and fragmentation of locality overview, to name a few.

How will we negotiate for the additional but essential services for primary care? We would be commissioning new workers, new skills into general practice to expand and extend care. If commissioning is the right term, there would have to be new money. One possibility is through enhanced services in GMS2 for depression.

There are many good examples of beacon systems to inspire primary care. The NICE Guidelines offer pragmatic help to prioritise and plan services for common mental health problems. Because they have the evidence base, we can use them as weapons to effect change. They give us strength in negotiating with tired managers and give us courage to change and confirm that changes do not have to be too radical to provide better care.

If PCTs are not willing to support a skilled, innovative service, then practices could consider taking on an indicative budget for mental health. Patient experience of care is still often unsatisfactory and patchy. I have anxieties about well-resourced practices alongside others where the provision is neither so varied nor cohesive; we are responsible for our locality not just our practice population.

There are two main decisions to be made. Will we commission at PCT level or will we do it at practice level? Will we commission for primary care services or will we commission secondary care services?

We may not have a choice but we are fingering the gauntlet.

PART FOUR

James Lind Alliance: identifying patients' and clinicians' priorities for therapeutic research

No commercial potential?
(nullus pretii)

Frank Arnold

What strategies can efficiently generate new treatments which benefit patients? One venerable method is to combine old knowledge of already existing drugs or devices with novel biomedical insights to find new uses for old remedies. This strategy has produced many successes (*see* Table A). It even has a new investor-friendly title: 'indication switching'.[1] Instances where it has (so far) failed are also worth examining, to identify obstacles to potentially useful biomedical research.

Table A Well known 'indication switches'

Drug	*First indication*	*New Indication*
Aspirin	pain/inflammation	cardio-vascular protection
Thalidomide	sedative (teratogen)	leprosy
Metronidazole	anti-protozoal	kills anaerobic bacteria
Hydrocolloid	dental drug delivery system	wound dressing
Morphine	systemic analgesic	topical analgesic
Amitryptiline	antidepressant	analgesic
Amoxycillin	antibiotic	peptic ulcers
AZT	cancer treatment (failed)	HIV
Nitrates	angina	anal fissure
Metformin	diabetes	polycystic ovary syndrome

Cromones may be a case in point. They are a textbook example of intelligent design by a single individual, Roger Altounyan, who used himself as a guinea pig to test the following hypothesis:

> Khellin, a plant traditionally used in the Middle East to make an infusion to treat asthma, contains active ingredients which can be purified and modified to create useful drugs.

Ultimately, after overcoming many obstacles, including outright obstruction by his employers, a pharmaceutical company, he was successful.[2] The best known result, cromoglycate (Intal), is widely used to reduce the frequency of asthma attacks in children. It must be (and is) very safe, and is delivered by a novel system, which he also invented.

Cromones (of which Intal is one) act, at least in part, by blocking the release of chemical signals by mast cells, which are involved in many allergic disorders. Mast cells are also thought to be important in cancer, largely by promoting the growth of the blood supply essential to tumour growth.

In 1983, on the basis of this information, colleagues and I did a small experiment to test the effects of Intal on the growth of cancers in mice. As we later discovered, we were neither the first nor the last to explore this potential. Between our initial experiments and the present day, five other groups have performed similar experiments, usually in apparent ignorance of previous work (*see* Table B). In addition, an Italian group conducted a small randomised controlled trial of Intal for palliation of intractable cough in patients with advanced bronchial cancers.[3]

So here we have an asthma drug of established safety, which just may have new and beneficial uses in cancer.

On four occasions over the period 1984–1992, I approached Fisons, who held the patents on cromones, with these results, seeking support for a human trial in advanced human cancers. The company finally agreed to fund a clinical study, but before it could be begun, Fisons was forced out of the pharmaceutical industry, and eventually sold its intellectual property to another firm.

On being approached with an improved proposal last year, the response of the second company was illuminating:

> ... we are not currently investing in any clinical trial programs with Intal for reasons I mentioned to you over the phone, i.e mature product, patent issues, commercial interest ... we are also conscious of the forthcoming EU Clinical Trials Directive (1 May 2004) which would have major impact on the way companies support investigator-led studies, and potentially make such small centre trials in the future impossible to do.

In brief, research on a treatment which may be beneficial and is almost certainly safe, could not be supported by industry because the patent on the drug had expired. Also, regulations designed to promote patient safety may prohibit it altogether.

Although it is difficult to quantify this problem, many conversations with clinical researchers, in industry and outside it, suggest that this is a common occurrence. As such, it deserves a name. With reference to the spirit of self-interested obscurantism which has often been a hallmark of the medical profession, we could perhaps give it a Latin tag. 'No Commercial Potential' translates as *Nullus Pretii*.

Can useful but unprofitable treatments be established without industrial support? The MRC and medical research charities have a proud record, but the proportion of clinical research funded outside industry is now relatively small and decreasing.[4]

It may be worth looking again at the commercially successful examples of 'indication switching' in Table A. Public support and demand can sometimes drive research priorities and implementation on a large scale – the obvious example is aspirin. But almost all the rest of these developments were driven by commercial imperatives – most notably Viagra.

The rules of the game are obvious, but worth restating. Private investment is only feasible if the manufacturing process, or delivery and use of a drug are, or can be, covered by patent. Lacking this, the Western pharmaceutical industry is generally unable to find new uses for old drugs.

This is a perverse outcome. Patent laws were developed initially to give inventors a reasonable reward for their initiatives, and in exchange, to ensure that the public would reap a common right to use this knowledge within reasonable time. The patent-based business model which has evolved in the pharmaceutical industry prevents the evaluation of potentially important new uses of out-of-patent drugs. It has also proved remarkably unsuccessful in developing new drugs which represent real therapeutic advances.[5]

As patients, and as those who care for them, this should concern us. It is generally safer, faster and cheaper to develop and distribute drugs whose absorption, distribution, metabolism and toxicity are already well known from widespread use, than to start with new chemical entities. Some of these indication switches may not be blockbusters – no sales of $1 billion per year for a few years. But they could become useful treatments for thousands of patients over many years.

This would require an alternative to the flawed business model of deliberate obsolescence of drugs, which is increasingly dependent on legal protectionism and marketing hype. The James Lind Initiative may be well placed to help build such an alternative.

Table B Cromones causing tumour growth restraint

Reference	Date	Species	Tumour	Model	Agent
6	1991	Rat	Mammary	Transplant	FPL 55618
7	1986	Rat	Skin	Carcinogen	Intal
8	1975	Mouse	Ascites	Transplant	Intal
9	1983	Mouse	Melanoma	Transplant	Proxicromil
10	1986	Rat	Sarcoma	Transplant	Proxicromil
11	1991	Mouse	Mammary	Transplant	Intal
12	1991	Rat	Mammary	Carcinogen	Intal

Competing interests

Frank Arnold is a director of, and holds shares in, Polymed Therapeutics Ltd, a company he established to develop diagnostics and treatments for problem wounds. He is also a doctor and (when this is unavoidable) a patient. As a recurrent failure at smoking cessation, he may eventually need palliative care for bronchogenic carcinoma.

References

1 www.propagate.com/capabilities/indication_switch.html. Accessed 24 November 2004.

2 Reynolds LA and Tansey EM (eds) (2001) *Childhood asthma and beyond.* Wellcome Witnesses to Twentieth Century Medicine, vol. 11. The Wellcome Trust Centre for the History of Medicine at UCL, London. www.ucl.ac.uk/histmed/PDFS/Publications/Witness /wit11.pdf Accessed 24 November 2004.

3 Moroni M, Porta C, Gualtieri G, Nastasi G and Tinelli C (1996) Inhaled sodium cromo-glycate to treat cough in advanced lung cancer patients. *British Journal of Cancer* **74**: 309–11.

4 Chalmers I, Rounding C and Lock K (2003) Descriptive survey of non-commercial randomised controlled trials in the United Kingdom, 1980–2002. *BMJ* **327**: 1017.

5 Hubbard T and Love J (2004) A New Trade Framework for Global Healthcare R&D. *PloS* **2**. www.plosbiology.org/plosonline/?request = get-document&doi = 10.1371%2Fjournal. pbio.0020052, accessed 24 November 2004.

6 Dabbous MK *et al.* (1991) Mast cell modulation of tumour cell proliferation in rat mammary adenocarcinoma 13762NF. *British Journal of Cancer* **63**: 873.

7 Vlckova A *et al.* (1986) The blocking effect of disodium cromoglycate on carcinogenesis induced by benzo(a)pyrene. *Carcinogenesis* **7**: 371.

8 Castelli M *et al.* (1975) Rapporti tra istamina e crescita tumorale. *Riv Farmacol Ter.* **6**: 237.

9 Nordlund J *et al.* (1983) The effect of histamine, antihistamines and a mast cell stabiliser on the growth of Cloudman melanoma cells in DBA/2 mice. *Journal of Investigative Dermatology* **81**: 28.

10 Roche WR (1986) The nature and significance of tumour associated mast cells. *J Pathol.* **148**: 175.

11 Arnold F *et al.* (1991) Cromoglycate: a benign anti-angiogenic therapy? *International Journal of Radiation Biology* **60**: 78.

12 Ionov I (1991) Inhibition of mast cell activity as a new approach to anti-cancer therapy. *International Journal of Radiation Biology* **60**: 287.

Therapeutic research into psoriasis: patients' perspectives, priorities and interests

Ray Jobling

My understanding, such as it is, rests on nearly 50 years of having and treating psoriasis and over 30 years of involvement in The Psoriasis Association.

Psoriasis is characterised by extended chronicity. It affects around 2% of the population and decades of continuous daily treatment are a not uncommon experience. Psoriasis patients encounter *breakthrough* after *breakthrough*, with fanfare and loud promise ending ultimately in disappointment. It is a challenging and frustrating disease, with only rarely risk to life but an insidious potential for damage to self-esteem, nagging anticipated threat of social rejection and debilitating distracting impairment of well-being and quality of life. Psoriasis patients are frequently reminded that they are not 'ill'. Whatever the intended meaning, they can be nonetheless 'ill at ease'.

In the absence of the ability to 'cure', dermatologists have often in the past seemed aimed for total clearance of lesions in plaque psoriasis, or as close as could be achieved, promising the prospect of remission. Failing this, the objective has been to reduce the 'severity' of the disease, via reduction of the extensiveness and/or thickness of plaques. Encountering failure, the routine has been to try again repeatedly, the patient urged ever more firmly to comply strictly, religiously, with the regime. Thereafter, after a laborious progression through a series of treatments, the aim was at least to contain the physical expression of the disease.

Selection of therapeutic options and assessment of their value clearly should have rested in all this upon a grounding of research findings and lessons learned in clinical experience. Recent examination of RCTs and other studies of psoriasis treatments, however, have found them sadly wanting.[1] Dermatological practice rests upon no really firm research evidential base. Evidence is weak at best, conflicting, or simply non-existent. Arguably it matters little, given marked differences in the way in which the treatment of psoriasis is conducted from centre to centre, and country to country. Treatment decisions reflect not the lead given by evidence, but cultural, social and organisational background; and crucially demonstrate the effectiveness of the marketing strategies of different pharmaceutical companies.

Of 226 RCTs of psoriasis management between 1977 and 2000 examined in the EDEN Survey, over 60% were sponsored by the pharmaceutical industry.[2] Few trials involved comparison of different options or looked at long-term management. The duration of studies is unconvincingly brief in the context of a disease of potentially near life-long chronicity. We seem to know reliably only that our treatments are better than nothing at all. Tellingly, researchers have completely ignored patient experience, views, preferences or satisfactions.

The systemic treatment of choice for severe psoriasis in numerous countries, methotrexate, was the focus of no RCT comparing it with other treatments. Nor has there been even a single placebo comparison. Since the EDEN Survey one study has recently compared it with cyclosporin, financed from Dutch Government funds.[3] The EDEN researchers discovered only two RCTs comparing two or more systemic treatments. Of course methotrexate and other systemics in psoriasis therapy have had no commercial/financial relevance for the interests of the industry. One is forced to conclude that the principal influence on the focus, direction and substance of research has been corporate concern for financial return.

Patients' interests have been badly represented. They have been let down by the research and clinical community, and the 'system' for funding research, which has relied almost completely on commercial concerns. The interests of the latter have been paramount, with the complicity of the researchers themselves. Regrettably too, they have persisted with methodologically suspect, indeed weak, research designs and instruments. The measurement of outcomes, i.e. the effectiveness, has involved over 40 different bases for 'scoring'.[2] The emphasis has continued to be on area of skin affected, plus weak notions of thickness, in defining 'severity' and improvement, employing an instrument almost wholly discredited (the so-called Psoriasis Area and Severity Index (PASI) scoring system), notably deficient in dealing with mild-to-moderate disease, which fails to differentiate the relevance of psoriasis on different sites on the body for patient impact. Is the face of no greater subjective psychosocial significance and relevance for well-being than the back, for example?

The palms of the hands and the soles of the feet receive intriguingly little attention in the research mainstream. This is not because of irrelevance to patient concerns. Clearly the implications can be significant. It has to be that those considerations are of less moment than the commercial unattractiveness of investing in research into the problem. Psoriasis of the genitalia cannot be regarded by anyone as trivial. Rather the reverse, it would seem to warrant close study of treatment options. Yet it is neglected in the research literature, and irrelevant in PASI scoring. Here again the industry has found no lure of financial return in the problem. Dermatologists continue to wrestle with guttate psoriasis. Given what is already known about it, it is disappointing to have such little interest in approaches and treatments 'upstream' as it were, attempting to address the provocative factors.

Finally, what of those forms or components of therapy which are alternatives or adjuncts to pharmacological intervention? Psychological techniques – cognitive and/or behavioural therapy, counselling, relaxation, group therapy and the like – have only recently come into research focus in any significant way. They are of little interest unless – and this is revealing – they are interpreted as devices for securing more reliable and complete patient loyalty and compliance with regimes employing pharmacological products.

What of patient concerns and preferences? Increasingly, questionnaire surveys have been employed. The best have contributed usefully to better understanding (e.g. the instruments developed in Cardiff and Salford, UK). Sadly, however, many leave much to be desired methodologically, and betray in focus, and very plainly in analysis and presentation of results, the influence of the marketing agencies commonly prompting them, albeit they may have sheltered behind legitimising 'fronts'. In this latter respect patient organisations have themselves been naive, seduced unwarily into 'disease awareness campaigns' and 'third-party' marketing campaigns, a growing feature of the industry's strategy.

There are, of course, opportunities to bring forward patient interests, and much could be gleaned from reinterpreting the findings of research, within frameworks different from those originally applied by its initiators. Recent efforts to explore the phenomenon of 'non-compliance' offer an example.[4] There is evidence speaking volumes about the realities of living with a chronic, maybe lifelong, disease like psoriasis and the treatment regimes applied to it. It illuminates attempts made by patients to come to a reasonable compromise between the demands of the disease and its treatment, and their entirely understandable desire to live as close to normal a life as possible. Sadly, commonly discussion of 'non-compliance' is still blighted by implicit victim-blaming, solely an attitudinal problem to be overcome rather than offering valuable insight into illness behaviour and the experience of treatment.

There is interesting research emerging which puts patient perceptions, beliefs, understandings and objectives at the centre of attention.[5] Thus we have had reminders that scaliness, itch, soreness and obtrusiveness, all of which of can be provoked by treatment itself, are of real importance to patients.[6] These are central to patients' *own* judgements of 'severity', neglected in the mainstream research literature. Wanting lasting improvement, patients are resistant to inconvenient treatment offering no more than transient benefit. They reject it when aware of side-effects causing short-term discomfort or, worse, long-term harm. It is not that they are unwilling to accept any degree of uncertainty in this latter regard, but increasingly they do expect appropriate briefing on the basis of known evidence; and genuine consultation, involvement and responsibility in decision making – the essential basis of concordance.

Some say we are entering a new exciting era in psoriasis therapy, promised by new systemic agents, the 'biologicals'. A race is on to capture the lucrative market offered by moderate-to-severe disease. The pace is fast, arguably needlessly reckless given that so little is known about the effectiveness of the older-fashioned drugs, let alone their comparative merits alongside these new agents. How justified are claims made for them when we have as yet no more than placebo-controlled RCTs, and no long-term studies of efficacy, side-effects, safety or patient experience, in closely monitored use for psoriasis?

Patients will need reassurance on these fronts, plus estimates of relapse rates on withdrawal, and forecasts of treatment failure. Yet patients' representatives have been once again largely excluded from constructive involvement in setting the research agenda, and from discussion in the early stages of this 'revolution' in treatment. An international 'consensus' conference convened earlier this year on the biologicals (by a company introducing one to market) benefited from no patient input, despite ranging over issues central to their concerns, e.g. efficacy, safety, quality of life, disability, patient goals, ability/willingness to 'comply', etc.[7] Patients were not present even to comment on the consensus arrived at on 'patient-related considerations' for use of a biological, or the dramatic guidance offered that, 'Treatment of psoriasis no longer requires a strict step-wise approach'. Other 'stakeholders' and their interests were represented. The terms of debate have clearly been set, but without any direct involvement of patients.

References

1   Naldi L, Svensson A, Diepgen T et al. (2003) Randomised clinical trials for psoriasis 1977–2000: the EDEN survey. *Journal of Investigative Dermatology* **120**: 738–41.

2   Chalmers JG and Griffiths CEM (2003) Commentary: Resetting the research agenda for psoriasis. *Journal of Investigative Dermatology* **120**: ix–x.

3   Heydendael VMR, Spuls PI, Opmeer BC et al. (2002) Effectiveness, safety, & quality of life of methotrexate versus cyclsporin A in moderate to severe psoriasis: A randomised controlled trial. *British Journal of Dermatology* **147**: 1058 (abstract).

4   Zagloul SS and Goodfield MJ (2004) Objective assessment of compliance with psoriasis treatment. *Archives of Dermatology* **140**: 408–14.

5   Errser S, Surridge H and Wiles A (2002) What criteria do patients use when judging the effectiveness of psoriasis management? *Journal of Evaluation in Clinical Practice* **8**: 367–76.

6   Van de Kerkhof PCM, de Hoop D, de Korte J et al. (2000) Patient compliance and disease management in the treatment of psoriasis in the Netherlands. *Dermatology* **200**: 292–98.

7   Sterry W, Barker J, Boehncke JD et al. (2004) Biological therapies in the systemic management of psoriasis: International Consensus Conference. *British Journal of Dermatology* **151**(Suppl.69): 3–17.

Involving the public in health technology assessment

Sandy Oliver

As the James Lind Alliance considers how to identify and prioritise research topics,[1] I would like to recommend drawing on descriptions of public involvement in research agenda setting in the international literature and experience of developing methods for these tasks within the National Health Service.

Models of public involvement

A systematic review[2] of published and unpublished literature found that models of public involvement differ in terms of whether they:

- involve individual patients or members of patient groups
- who are consulted occasionally or involved in an ongoing collaborative relationship and
- are instigated either by researchers or the public.

These working relationships can occur in:

- a choice of settings for exchanging ideas
- with formal or informal methods for reaching decisions and
- with a variety of training and support for everyone.

Learning from different models of public involvement

This review found that typically during its first decade the NHS Research and Development's National Programmes involved one or two members of patient organisations in Advisory Committees setting research agendas. Even though these committees reflected on their working methods and their products, there was usually little or no reflection on public involvement, no records of the public's views and few lessons learnt, if any, about public involvement.

Town meetings offer a forum for public involvement on a larger scale. For instance, in the USA the National Institute for Occupational Safety and Health held town meetings in Chicago, Boston and Seattle that involved health professionals, researchers, organised labour, workers, businesses, service users, state and local health officials, elected officials and the general public.[3] Yet again, there was no published reflection on public involvement and no record of the public's views.

Far more has been learnt about patients' views using conventional social research methods. One-to-one and group interviews with arthritis patients and the use of questionnaires identified the treatments patients had tried and the treatments they considered deserved more research: all treatments, including education and advice, physical therapy and complementary therapy.[4] However, this approach did not include patients in decisions about research to be conducted.

A more inclusive approach is participatory or action research which includes collaboration, education and action. Such research stresses the relationship between researcher and community, with the direct benefit to the community as an outcome of the research and the community's involvement as itself beneficial. Where young people from low income families in California have been supported by academics to do their own research, they have chosen to address local issues: pollution in a bay where their families fished, the lack of youth recreation places, library closures, alcoholism in the home and local environmental politics.[5] Participatory research has also been undertaken with subsistence farmers in Kenya. When trained through discovery-based learning to choose topics and carry out their own research, they addressed soil pest and disease management for nursery beds, and the use of milk sprays to control leaf diseases in tomato.[6]

It appears that, whatever the model of involvement, more has been learnt about people's priorities where they have had a leading role in consulting their peers and where their reflections on the methods of their involvement have been recorded and published.

Whatever the model, public involvement in research agenda setting requires asking people for their ideas, sharing and discussing those ideas and making decisions. Each of these steps can be either formal or informal. Very little is known about how ideas are discussed or decisions made, or what methods work best, largely because reports rarely include such details.

Developing public involvement in HTA

The HTA programme, which commissioned the systematic review, is setting an example by reporting how it has developed and evaluated public involvement in its work. It has tried a range of methods to involve members of patient and public organisations in identifying and prioritising topics before commissioning research.[7] The programme has employed a cycle of development that starts with inviting public representatives in each aspect of its work, seeking feedback, developing procedures and resources to enhance their involvement and refining these in light of feedback again.[8]

The programme evaluates its work by asking: what do people think about public involvement; what do the public contribute to the research programme; and how do the public influence the research programme?

Public contributions to HTA

Some comments from the public on briefings about research need and on research proposals have focused on those people included in research and those excluded. Others address the interventions being evaluated and their social context; perhaps suggesting alternatives or combinations for evaluation, or commenting on the acceptability of an intervention. They suggest outcomes for assessment such as coping, social and emotional well-being, harmful outcomes, long-term outcomes, and outcomes highlighted as important by patients. Their comments on study methods focus directly on the participating patients, their willing participation, informed consent, advocacy and monitoring patient experiences; and on methods for active public involvement to guide the study.

Public influence of HTA

Close scrutiny of routine management records is revealing examples of public influence as well as public involvement. When a briefing of research need was being prepared about the 'burden on family members' with frail elderly people, it was a member of a charity who pointed out that any evaluation should address the needs of those receiving support from their family and elsewhere as well as the needs of the family. This was incorporated into the research commissioning brief. A more detailed comment from the same person questioning whether a 'quality of life' measure adequately evaluated both social and psychological problems was not incorporated.

Similarly, when a health professional invited to comment on the same research briefing wrote that, of all the interventions for people with dementia, 'the most concrete intervention in which guidance is potentially important is respite care', the brief was changed from the broader focus of 'burden on family members' to a more specific focus on 'respite care'. But more detailed suggestions from a health professional about 'important sub groups' such as carers of people with dementia compared with those who have a physical condition, and distinguishing those cared for by a spouse, the younger generation or a neighbour, was not incorporated into the brief.

What we know and what we don't

From the emerging findings of this work we know that, like clinicians and researchers, members of the public *can* make pertinent comments on health technology assessment, and their comments *can* influence commissioned research. However, we don't know whether members of the public *often* make pertinent comments about HTA, whether comments from the public *often* influence commissioned research or whether comments from the public *differ* from clinicians' or researchers' comments.

More research is needed to find the most efficient points in managing a commissioned programme to involve the public, and the cost-benefit balance of public involvement.

Acknowledgements

I have drawn on work funded by The Nuffield Trust, the National Coordinating Centre for Health Technology Assessment, and the NHS Health Technology Assessment programme. This work was conducted with Jane Royle, David Armes, Gill Gyte, Rebecca Rees, Lorna Clarke-Jones, Ruairidh Milne, John Gabbay, Ann Oakley and Ken Stein.

References

1   Anonymous (2004) Confronting important uncertainties about the effects of treatments: the James Lind Alliance. *Health and Social Campaigners' News* **5**.

2   Oliver S, Clarke-Jones L, Rees R, Milne R, Buchanan P, Gabbay J, Gyte G, Oakley A and Stein K (2004) Involving consumers in Research and development Agenda setting for the NHS: developing an evidence-based approach. *Health Technology Assessment* **8**(15): 1–148.

3   Rosenstock L, Olenec C and Wagner GR (1998) The National Occupational Research Agenda: A model of broad stakeholder input into priority setting. *American Journal of Public Health* **88**: 353–6.

4   Tallon D, Chard J and Dieppe P (2000) Relation between agendas of the research community and the research consumer. *The Lancet* **355**(9220): 2037–40.

5   Schwab M (1997) Sharing power: participatory public research with California teens. *Social Justice* **24**(3): 11–32.

6   Kimani M, Mihindo N and Williamson S (undated) *We too are proud to be researchers: Farmer participatory training and research in traditional pest and disease management in Kenya.* CABI Bioscience (unpublished).

7   Oliver S, Milne R, Bradburn J, Buchanan P, Kerridge L, Walley T and Gabbay J (2001) Involving consumers in a needs-led research programme: a pilot project. *Health Expectations* **4**(1): 18–28.

8   Royle J and Oliver S (2004) Consumer involvement in the health technology assessment programme. *International Journal of Health Technology Assessment in Health Care* **20**(4): 493–7.

Identifying patients' and clinicians' priorities in cancer clinical trials

Hazel Thornton

In order to identify patients' and clinicians' priorities in cancer clinical trials, there are two main requirements: a climate conducive for doing it; and processes and systems for bringing it about.

The most important thing to have changed since my first published patient's viewpoint on breast cancer trials in January 1992[1] is the attitude of many committed health professionals. This means that informed patients[2] now have increasing opportunities to work together with health professionals to have a say in research affairs, including prioritisation of topics for research. The Cochrane Collaboration has welcomed and encouraged patient participation from its beginning in 1992. The Royal Colleges, the MRC and other institutions have set up Consumer Liaison Groups. The NHS, itself, established a 'Consumers in Research' initiative in 1995. *Health Expectations* published its first issue in 1998 and has become a respected international journal covering public participation in healthcare and health policy.

My own group, jointly founded with Professor Michael Baum, was the Consumers' Advisory Group for Clinical Trials (CAG-CT).[3,4] It was set up in 1994. This was a working group of health professionals, and breast cancer patients, seeking to bridge the gaps between patients, clinicians and researchers. Our second aim was to advance public education about clinical trials. We saw ourselves as 'facilitators for progress', and committed to finding ways of working collaboratively to improve research methodologies. By this sharing of responsibility we sought to promote a new attitude to research, devised in a spirit of cooperation[5] so that it would be relevant to patients.

We started with a research project, and feasibility study, funded by the NHS Research & Development Programme.[6] This work informed a multi-centre trial of HRT in women with early breast cancer.[7] In this project, independently facilitated focus groups were used to identify and prioritise the desired outcomes of patients, researchers and clinicians. The findings are included in the trial protocol. It also identified the specific training needs for those who would run the trial and the information needs of the participants, patients[8] and health professionals. The focus groups had clear ground rules for deriving priorities, enabling equitable input from a very mixed group of researchers, clinicians, patients and advocates.[9,10]

I want to emphasise that, in this project, the breast cancer patient/ researchers undertook this work, not through personal interest use of HRT after a diagnosis of breast cancer, but because they recognised that there was a general high level of uncertainty about this in the community. They recognised that clinicians, and many patients with breast cancer (with extreme menopausal symptoms as a result of the treatment), were confused and uncertain about the use of HRT and the effects of tamoxifen. Exploration of this topic by qualitative research methods also exposed many misunderstandings on the part of both patients and clinicians, and was thus mutually educative.

Such patient advocates, working very closely with experienced clinicians in a facilitative working group, are able to develop a professional detachment that, although founded on personal experience of the disease, puts aside personal considerations in order to address general uncertainties. They appreciate the benefit that could accrue in terms of quality of life to many thousands of fellow-sufferers, from testing a hypothesis in a controlled fashion.

These principles were used in the Health in Partnership study of shared decision-making. The CAG-CT was involved from the pre-trial phase. In this work, focus group participants identified many affective outcomes that were consistent with current literature trends. However, many cognitive and behavioural outcomes that had been assessed in the literature were not thought to be important by the focus group participants. Importantly, a broader range of outcomes than was evident in the literature of the time was viewed as important.

Roles are evolving, and can evolve even in the course of a research project.[11] Increasingly, various categories of 'consumers' are being involved with researchers in pre-trial qualitative research. This type of work can explore the feasibility, acceptability and relevance of a hypothesis.[12] In the Welsh study of shared decision-making and risk communication,[13] consumers and patients were involved in the development and validation of an instrument (COMRADE) that addressed the range of outcomes identified by users as important, even though they might be difficult to measure.[14] If delivery of patient-centre healthcare is to become a reality, it is vital to know what citizens value most when they become patients, and to be able to measure these accurately and reliably.

These types of engagements demand, from both involved user and health professional, an approach that is in tune with contemporary society and the newly evolved patient-centred culture.[15,16] Perceptions about involving users are not always flattering or accurate, and need reshaping and redefining. Users are becoming increasingly involved with health professionals in activities that aim to bring improvements in healthcare delivery.[17] The doctor–patient relationship is undergoing change: research findings inform and guide development of this new-style partnership more suited to today's attitudes and aspirations.[18–21,11] Medical research and related activities now involve recipients of healthcare, from inception of hypotheses to dissemination and systematic reviewing of accumulating evidence. Committees, conference-planning groups, research project steering committees and other organisational medical activities are no longer the sole preserve of health professionals. Users are no longer 'outsiders'.[22] The patient is now recognised as possessing unique expertise and experience that can enhance deliberations, provide insights and valuable contributions formally and informally, both in one-to-one exchanges and in structured situations.

Delivery of patient-centred care requires evidence about interventions that improve patients' quality of life. Many of the breast cancer trials listed for the 8th National Breast Cancer Trials Meeting in November 2004 had a quality of life component. There is also a new section listing 'Management of Care' studies.[23] But there is a need to increase the role of patients and clinicians, working together, to shape the therapeutic research agenda, and to use new models of engagement. Health professionals and patients are best placed to be able to identify and order the priorities for research about topics that matter to patients. Ways are being found to encourage full engagement between clinicians and patients both in healthcare provision and in research.[24] This engagement can take place at many levels (individual or group) and in many ways. The UK leads the way in promoting this collaboration in the research process from pre-trial through to dissemination and implementation: many models are available on the database of the NHS organisation for consumers in research: INVOLVE.[25]

We can now extend this collaboration by encouraging partnerships between organisations representing patients, and organisations representing clinicians, working together to confront important uncertainties about the effects of treatments, within the James Lind Alliance.[26]

References

1 Thornton HM (1992) Viewpoint: Breast cancer trials: the patient's viewpoint. *The Lancet* **339**: 44–5.

2 Thornton H (2004) 'The informed patient'. *Journal of Royal College of Physicians of Edinburgh* **34**: 124–9.

3 National Centre for Clinical Audit (1998) Consumers' Advisory Group for Clinical Trials: its genesis. *NCCA Newsletter*. **8 May 1998**.

4 Thornton H (2001) Information and Involvement. *Health Expectations* **4**(1): 71–4.

5 Thornton H (1993) A 'ladyplan' for trial recruitment – everyone's business! (editorial). *The Lancet* **341**: 795–6.

6 NHS Research and Development Programme (Cancer) (1995) *Using a consumers advisory group to increase accrual into Trials*. Project NCP/D18. London Institute of Cancer Research: London.

7   The Institute of Cancer Research (2002) *UK Randomised Trial of Hormone Replacement Therapy (HRT) in Women with a History of Early Stage Breast Cancer.* The Institute of Cancer Research: Sutton.

8   Breast Cancer, Hormones & HRT: A booklet for patients and those close to them. Written by a committee of patients and healthcare professionals working together under the chairmanship of Dr Jane Maher. 1998; revised 2002. Lynda Jackson Macmillan Centre for Cancer Support and Information. Mount Vernon Hospital: Northwood.

9   Marsden J and Bradburn J (2004) Patient and clinician collaboration in the design of a national randomised breast cancer trial. *Health Expectations* 7: 6–17.

10   Thornton H (2004) Reporting dates is necessary to establish historical perspective – and validity of references (letter). *Health Expectations* 7: 268.

11   Thornton H, Edwards A and Elwyn G (2003) Evolving the multiple rôles of 'patients' in healthcare research: reflections after involvement in a trial of shared decision-making. *Health Expectations* 6(3): 189–97.

12   Thornton H and Dixon-Woods M (2002) Recruitment of women into trials. *The Lancet* **359**: 164.

13   Edwards A, Elwyn G, Atwell C *et al.* (2002) *Shared decision making and risk communication in general practice – a study incorporating systematic literature reviews, psychometric evaluation of outcome measures, and quantitative, qualitative and health economic analysis of a cluster randomised trial of professional skill development.* Report to 'Health in Partnership' programme, UK Department of Health. Department of General Practice, University of Wales College of Medicine: Cardiff. www.healthinpartnership.org/studies/edwards.html

14   Chalmers I and Clarke M (2001) Outcomes that matter to patients in tombstone trials. *The Lancet* **358**: 1649.

15   Irvine D (2004) Professionalism: dead or alive? (book review). *The Lancet* **364**: 1479–80.

16   Mark Walport, Director of the Wellcome Trust, speaking early in 2004. Quoted by The Scientist: see www.biomedcentral.com/news/20040623/03, accessed 28/10/04.

17   Hanley B, Truesdale A, King A, Elbourne D and Chalmers I (2001) Involving consumers in designing, conducting, and interpreting randomised controlled trials: questionnaire survey. *BMJ* **322**: 519–23.

18   Donovan J, Mills N, Brindle L, Frankel S, Smith M, Jacoby A *et al.* (2002) Improving the design and conduct of randomised trials by embedding them in qualitative research: the ProtecT study. *BMJ* **325**: 766–69.

19   Koops L and Lindley R (2002) Thrombolysis for acute ischaemic stroke: consumer involvement in design of new randomised controlled trials. *BMJ* **325**: 415–17.

20   Dixon-Woods M, Agarwal S, Young B, Jones D and Sutton A (2004) *Integrative approaches to qualitative and quantitative evidence.* Report for NHS Health Development Agency. www.had.nhs.uk

21   Edwards A, Elwyn G, Smith C, Williams S and Thornton H (2001) Consumers' views of quality in the consultation and their relevance to 'shared decision-making' approaches. *Health Expectations* 4(3): 151–60.

22 Refractor (2000) 'Insiders' and 'outsiders' in research collaborations? *The Lancet* **356**: 1038.

23 'Current National Trials'. NCRI 8th National Breast Cancer Trials Meeting. 17 November 2004. Institute of Cancer Research: Sutton.

24 Coulter A and Rozansky D (2004) Full engagement in health. *BMJ* **329**: 1197–8.

25 NHS Consumers in Research: INVOLVE. www.invo.org.uk, see: Database of research projects.

26 The James Lind Alliance. www.lindalliance.org

PART FIVE

Getting governance right

Do NHS structural issues hamper R&D?

Marc Taylor

Introduction

Structural change in the NHS is bound to affect the way we organise ourselves around R&D. We can expect more change, designed to

- strengthen joint working with our partners
- build infrastructure for more and better clinical research and public health R&D
- harmonise working practices and
- encourage good research.

Recent changes shifted the balance between the DH and the NHS. Before 2004, over 100 people worked on R&D for the Department. A third of them came in from the previous regional structure. They focused mainly on supporting the NHS, and on performance management. Their task in the 1990s was to set up managed systems for the NHS R&D Budget. From 2001, they focused on governance and quality issues.

Meanwhile, research-active bodies in health and social care were establishing their own R&D offices. Increasingly, they use joint offices, or share expertise through networks. They have created vehicles to share best practice, such as the NHS R&D Forum, the association of teaching hospitals, and the research management network of PCTs.

In 2003, the DH regional structure was removed. Since 2004, Sally Davies, the DH Director of R&D, has had a Directorate of 50 posts within the Standards and Quality Group headed by the Chief Medical Officer (CMO): see Figure A.

When the new team is complete, it will cover:

- research strategy, policy and governance
- liaison with the NHS, with industry and with other partners
- parliamentary and corporate business and communications
- national research programmes

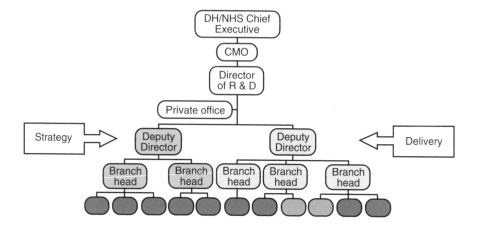

Figure A The new Research and Development Directorate

- health and social care organisations' research programmes
- planning and management of the national R&D budget.

Why do we have research governance?

Since before the NHS was created, health ministers have had broad powers to commission research, and to facilitate others' research. These powers and duties are now part of the legal basis of the NHS.

It is in the interest of patients and the public to understand the patterns and causes of disease, to promote innovation in health and social care, and have access to high-quality evidence about the effectiveness of treatments.

Research relies on partnerships with others, such as universities, charities and other research funders, and industry. The Research Governance Framework sets out what health and social care organisations should expect of their partners, and what partners should expect of health and social care.

An explicit standard for research governance reassures those who consent to take part in research that health and social care organisations know how to protect their safety, rights, dignity and well-being.

Why integrate research governance into risk management?

Research governance is not separate from other duties that health and social care organisations have towards their patients, service users, carers, staff and other individuals who could suffer harm.

NHS bodies have a legal Duty of Quality. In July 2004, the Department issued a set of standards relating to that duty, called *Standards for Better Health*. Research governance is one of the core standards (Figure B).

Most of the risks in research can be managed through systems that handle the same risk outside research. These are linked to internationally recognised quality systems and principles of good clinical practice.

Because of this, there will be an integrated system of performance assessment, review and inspection run by the Healthcare Commission. It will include research governance. A consultation about it is under way.

The DH issued a second edition of the Research Governance Framework in 2005.

What should we expect of SHAs, PCTs and NHS Trusts?

Partners' R&D needs NHS permission. NHS bodies are expected to manage risk and minimise bureaucratic processes. We should help good research to succeed, as well as turning away studies that are not ready to start.

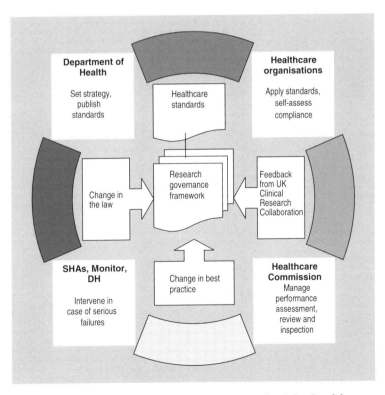

Figure B Using research governance as a core standard for health care

NHS scrutiny should be proportionate, timely and focused on the body's own responsibilities. In general, we should rely on reasonable assurances from others, and not second-guess them in carrying out their own duties. Better networking could make NHS processes more consistent and user-friendly.

For research initiated for the NHS, we could do much more to promote high-quality studies. The NHS needs to build up infrastructure for clinical trials, helped by the new UK Clinical Research Collaboration. It needs to make robust arrangements for sponsorship. It needs to set aside expert time for leadership of R&D, and build up academic partnerships to raise quality.

Audit: does it work and is it worth the effort?

John Holden

Audit is one of the longest quality improvement methods in the NHS. Indeed, it predates it and, most famously, Florence Nightingale developed methods of auditing hospital care in the 19th century. More locally to me in South Lancashire is this epitaph of a general practitioner.

> *Sacred to the memory of James Jameson, of Ashton, Surgeon*
> *Who died in the 41st year of his Age*
> *In medical skill he had few equals*
> *In attention to the sick none excelled him*
> *Honest to the rich He never gave them too much medicine*
> *Kind to the poor he never gave them too little*
> *An ornament to his Profession*
> *He lived respected and died regretted*

From this we can see that the quality of care has long been of concern to practitioners, those they serve, and wider society. Out of this concern grew in the 20th century the Confidential Inquiries into Maternal Deaths, for many years the principle British example of a systematic attempt to improve patient care.

1990 NHS reforms

These reforms led to the widespread introduction of audit across the NHS, accompanied by substantial investment. This included the expenditure of £220 million over the next five years, of which 80% went to hospitals. Alan Maynard pithily commented, 'the Government is pouring money into the black hole of medical audit'.

In general practice Medical Audit Advisory Groups (MAAGs) were formed with a wide but vague brief to involve all GPs in audit. They depended upon local enthusiasts supported by a small number of staff. After five years a review[1] concluded, 'the flexibility of the original advisory group brief seems to have served many districts well, enabling the development of locally acceptable arrangements that would be difficult to specify in national legislation'.

What is audit?

But it is easy to assume there is agreement about what audit is. The term 'audit' is used quite loosely and almost any quality improvement scheme could be covered by some of the descriptions. The major divisions are between:

1 significant event audit – a review of individual cases or incidents in order to learn wider lessons
2 survey – a data collection exercise undertaken to establish the extent to which a policy or management plan is being achieved ('Are we doing what we intend to do?') and
3 audit cycle(s) – a process which involves an initial survey, setting standards and altering care, and a resurvey to demonstrate improvement. This audit-cycle, which can continue indefinitely, could include the evidence of the achievement of the childhood vaccination and immunisation targets in general practice, or any other target such as maximum waiting times for surgery.

However almost all 'audits' are actually a mixture of different interventions to improve performance (*see* Table A).

Table A Different interventions to improve performance

Educational materials	Opinion leadership	Peer-group meetings
Feedback of performance	Guidelines (external	Formularies
Meetings (local or	or local)	
in-practice)	Job redesign	Service redesign
Facilitator to practices	Target setting	Disease register production
Comparative data	Practice planning	External data collection
Reminders in records	Money (e.g. PGEA)	Other incentives
'Academic detailing'	Review of patient care	
	by clinicians	

It is surprisingly rare to get 'pure audit'. This was demonstrated in my review of the 48 multi-practice audits published from British general practice.[2]

The cost of audit

The direct costs are most obviously financial, but perhaps more expensive is the cost of professional time in collecting, analysing and discussing the results. This implies an opportunity cost – the other activities that may have been done in place of audit.

The benefits of audit

'As an educational experience, a good system of medical audit is worth any number of postgraduate courses'.[3] McWhinney predicted the conclusions of many audits over the next 30 years. Education was the principal benefit that St Helens MAAG members' identified as the group in 2001.

Improved patient care would be the purpose of most audits and, indeed, my review showed a typical project could do so by the order of 20%.[2] This would accord with a Cochrane review[4] that audit is of modest but variable effectiveness.

Is audit worth it?

And how his audit stands – who knows, save heaven?

Hamlet

A continued problem remains that of participation. Only 23% of the published general practice audits recruited 50% or more of local practice and, in St Helens, we concluded[5] that only 38% of practices were willing, regular participants in audit by 2000. Audit, however, remains a major part of efforts to improve patient care, as demonstrated by the posters displayed from across the UK at the 2004 NICE Conference. Although audit is expensive in time and effort, it is far less so than poor patient care.

Details of 'Fellowship by Assessment', a scheme for GPs to demonstrate high standards of care across many aspects of practice, can be found on the RCGP website.

References

1   Humphrey C and Berrow D (1995) Promoting audit in primary care; roles and relationships of medical audit advisory groups and their managers. *Quality in Health Care* **4**: 166–73.

2   Holden JD (2004) Systematic review of published multi-practice audits from British general practice. *Journal of Evaluation in Clinical Practice* **10**: 247–72.

3   McWhinney IR (1972) Medical audit in North America. *BMJ* **309**: 1340–2.

4   Thomson O'Brien MA, Oxman AD, Davis DA, Haynes RB, Freemantle N and Harvey EL (2001) Audit and feedback: effects on professional practice and health care outcomes [Cochrane Review]. In: *The Cochrane Library*, 2001, Issue 3. Update Software: Oxford.

5   Holden J and Sandys M (2001) Diffusion of the innovation of audit in a district: which practices and how far? *Journal of Clinical Governance* **9**: 133–5.

How new regulatory structures underpin accountability within integrated and multidisciplinary teams: the role of CHRE

Julie Stone

Introduction

Two significant regulatory developments have been the creation of the General Social Care Council (GSCC), and the establishment of the Council for Healthcare Regulatory Excellence (CHRE). The GSCC will regulate, for the first time, social workers and social care workers. CHRE will oversee the functions, and promote regulatory excellence, amongst the nine statutory healthcare regulators in the UK. The creation of these new bodies is particularly significant given the Government's commitment to strengthening links between health and social care. This paper will explore how current regulatory processes support integrated and multidisciplinary working.

CHRE functions

CHRE was established by the National Health Service Reform and the Healthcare Professions Act 2002 (under the statutory name of the Council for the Regulation of Healthcare Professionals). CHRE's functions are:

- to promote the interests of patients and other members of the public in the performance of their functions by regulators
- to promote best practice in regulation
- to promote principles of good, professionally led regulation
- to promote cooperation between the regulatory bodies and between them and bodies performing corresponding functions.

Critically, CHRE does not regulate practitioners. Rather, it oversees the functions of those that do. CHRE is committed to identifying and encouraging best practice in regulation, eventually working towards a regulatory system which achieves excellence consistently across the range of regulated professions. Increasingly, this will involve strengthening links between regulators and employers to ensure that workplace learning, for example, is encouraged and supported by them. Regulation also needs to be sufficiently flexible to support new ways of working including working across professional boundaries and the creation of new professional roles.

Ensuring accountability: individually and collectively

Being accountable is a key component of professionalism. Principally, professionals are accountable to those they serve – namely, the public. Patients assume that anyone tasked with caring for them will be qualified, competent and trustworthy. Individual accountability requires practitioners to maintain the highest levels of personal probity, to keep their knowledge and skills up-to-date, to adhere to codes of practice and ethics, and to work within the limits of their competence.

Collectively, regulatory bodies support accountability through their core functions: this includes maintaining a register of professionals, setting standards for education and training, requiring continuing professional development (CPD) and/or revalidation, providing guidance on standards and ethics, having fitness-to-practise mechanisms and communicating with the public about what they do. CHRE is working with regulators to promote best practice in each of these areas. It achieves this by way of an annual performance review process, by regular cross-regulatory forums and review, and by its consideration of each of the regulator's fitness-to-practise determinations.

Where desirable, CHRE promotes consistency in regulation if this is necessary to protect the public. This is important for public confidence, because patients already assume that all professionals who treat them work within a similarly exacting framework. The move towards greater consistency in key regulatory functions such as competency-based education and standards also supports integrated ways of working and the creation of new roles, as well as informing the public of what they can expect of their practitioners.

Professional regulation in the wider regulatory context

Professionally led regulation is only one aspect part of a broader regulatory framework aimed at creating excellence and accountability in the workplace. Health professionals are subject to a raft of regulatory and legislative controls.

Bodies with some form of regulatory function include employers, the Health Care Commission, the NHS complaints system, the NCAA, the National Patient Safety Agency (NPSA) and, indeed, NICE. Each of these different mechanisms needs to be more closely aligned to ensure that problems are identified early and that steps can be taken to prevent reoccurrence.

Part of CHRE's function is to promote cooperation between the regulatory bodies and other bodies performing corresponding functions. Ideally, this will help to promote a culture of shared learning from mistakes, whether identified by way of an NHS complaint, a Healthcare Commission inspection, an NPSA finding or a regulator's fitness-to-practise investigation. Learning would optimally be fed back into professional training and development, into professional codes issued by regulatory bodies, into employment protocols and into National Service Frameworks. This would generate a system of continuous improvement across service delivery as a whole.

Regulating individuals versus regulating teams

Historically, professional-led regulation has been focused on the individual registrant (although the regulatory bodies for opticians and pharmacists also regulate bodies corporate). The creation of strong, individual professions has for 150 years been seen as the appropriate way of ensuring excellence, by instilling in registrants the values and ethos of each given profession. In the current climate, however, the emphasis of modern, professional-led regulation is public protection, with lay people having a significant say in how professions should be regulated. It is increasingly hard to justify inconsistent regulatory arrangements across different professions when the same task could, for example, be performed by a nurse, a junior doctor, a social worker or a specially trained healthcare assistant.

Healthcare regulation is not expressly designed in a way which supports and facilitates integrated ways of working. Rather, it is implicitly assumed that practitioners who espouse professional principles and values will bring these strengths to integrated and multidisciplinary teams. Increasingly, regulatory bodies are looking at regulating different members of the team. The General Dental Council (GDC), for example, will shortly regulate professions complementary to dentistry as well as dentists. The focus on fitness-to-practise will, however, continue to be linked to individuals, not teams. If patients are to be optimally protected, systems of registration and accountability will need to keep pace with working across professional boundaries.

Common codes

Professionals can work together more readily if they are working to similar professional standards. Although the skills needed by different professions vary, there is a significant degree of commonality in the standards required of health-care professions. CHRE is working with regulators to ensure that professional codes set out similarly stringent requirements in areas such as respect for patients' autonomy, confidentiality, honesty and trustworthiness, maintaining professional boundaries, working within the limits of one's competence, and reporting poor performance of colleagues. In this respect it is notable that the Health Professions Council, which currently regulates 13 distinct professions, has a code of ethics which is largely common to all (with minor profession-specific variations where appropriate). This may serve as a template for bringing together systems of registration across a broader range of health professions.

Multi/inter-professional learning and development

Given the commonality discussed above, regulators clearly need to consider whether there is increasing scope for multiprofessional or inter-professional learning. Such learning could do much to break down the 'silos' between separate professions. This might include shared learning in areas such as ethics, law, communication and IT. CHRE will continue to work with regulators to ensure that practitioners admitted onto a professional register are suitably qualified to work in the modern healthcare workforce.

Regulatory challenges

As new ways of working continue to evolve and old hierarchies break down, regulation must strive to deliver a flexible and skilled workforce which can adapt to change. Integrated and multidisciplinary working is already the norm in many different settings. As demographics change, both the general population and within the healthcare workforce, changing professional roles are inevitable. CHRE will work in partnership with the regulators to ensure that regulated professionals continue to be fit for purpose. The professional values of excellence and accountability which underpin professionally led regulation remain unchanged.

The impact of stakeholders on the NICE guideline development process

Henny Pearmain

Introduction

This 10-month project *Enhancing stakeholder involvement in NICE guideline development: learning lessons from the allied health professions, health visiting, midwifery and nursing*, carried out in 2004, was initiated by the Clinical Effectiveness Forum for Allied Health Professions (CEFAHP), a subsidiary group of the Allied Health Professions Federation.

The project was funded by NICE in response to issues expressed by CEFAHP about the resource requirements of stakeholding. It was a collaborative study between 15 professional bodies representing the allied health professions, health visiting, midwifery and nursing. The 500 000 + members of these organisations represent two-thirds of staff responsible for direct patient care in the NHS. This explains the professional bodies investment in stakeholding and prime concern with usability of the clinical guidelines.

Project objectives

The project objectives are to:

- clarify the current process of stakeholder involvement in the development of NICE guidelines from the perspective of some professional stakeholders
- review the influence and impact of these professional stakeholders upon the guideline development process
- make recommendations about more efficient and effective ways in which professional stakeholders can contribute to the NICE guideline development process.

Methods

Two questionnaires were designed to gather information from professional body coordinators and experts about organisational systems and individual involvement in the stakeholder process.

Interviews were held to explore perceptions of the impact of professional stakeholders on the completed guidelines with those above and with staff from the NCCs, to give a balanced perspective.

The project concluded with a two-part consultation phase. A consultation draft of the report sought feedback about the merit and feasibility of the preliminary recommendations. A seminar then provided an interactive format to develop the key messages arising from the whole project.

Results

Most professional bodies had invested considerable resources in stakeholder relations. For example, six had incorporated NICE activities within their business plan.

Expert members who comment on draft documents on behalf of their profession matched this organisational investment. Most of the 38 experts held clinical posts in the NHS in England. Whilst many described their employer as fully supportive, most responded to the consultation drafts in their own time.

Some professional bodies did not get beyond the registration stage or had to limit their involvement. This was due to the lack of infrastructure resources to cope with the logistics of consultations; limited capacity or responses from expert members; or because the organisation gave priority to direct member services.

Most participants were more than satisfied with the stakeholder process. It was seen as an unprecedented opportunity to influence the quality of healthcare. However, there was increasing disappointment with the negligible influence of the allied health professions, health visiting, midwifery and nursing on the published guidelines. A complex set of reasons were given for the lack of impact. For example, the failure of the guidelines to signpost the particular skills offered by different professions and the lesser value given to qualitative studies and practitioner knowledge.

Prioritising three key messages

The main messages that arose from the consultation seminar were:

- Valuing:
  - all contributions equally regardless of the size, status or power of the profession

  - qualitative as well as quantitative research designs, and other sources of evidence such as practitioner knowledge
  - usability so that guidelines become a routine, relevant tool for quality improvement by all practitioners.
- Being heard:
  - by clarifying the purpose of stakeholding and ensuring consistency about nominations for the guideline development groups (GDG) and the use of expert advisors
  - through more two-way communication between stakeholders, NICE and the NCCs about practical and strategic matters, such as the topics selected for guidelines
  - by promoting research capacity to develop the evidence base for these research emergent professions.
- Streamlining resource demands:
  - through continued collaboration between professional bodies on subjects such as accrediting experts for the continued professional development gained as a stakeholder
  - by sharing learning, operational systems and resources amongst organisations via an informal network of professional body coordinators
  - providing financial support – such as honoraria and resources tailored to the different needs of stakeholders for specific guidelines, especially smaller professional bodies with minimal infrastructure and reliant upon volunteers.

Recommendations and suggested actions

These messages are manifest in the recommendations derived from the study that are targeted at the professional bodies, NICE and the NCCs. The 10 recommendations and 50 supplementary actions identify what needs to be done, often requiring the cooperation of different organisations. Some recommendations focus upon operational details, such as improving the systems for recruiting and supporting expert members. The strategic recommendations reflect the desire of professional bodies to be more than peer reviewers and to engage in a dialogue about ways of enhancing the usability of national clinical guidelines, such as the use of more person-focused language rather than simply the 'management of conditions'.

The challenge will be to foster the collaboration and goodwill generated by this project and to accommodate change so that stakeholders can really add their distinctive practice-based knowledge to the science of guideline development.

Acknowledgements

CEFAHP would like to thank NICE for funding the study, the steering group and the project team: Judy Mead (project manager) and Ralph Hammond (advisor) from the Chartered Society of Physiotherapy; Julia Roberts (coordinator) from the College of Occupational Therapists; and the lead researcher Dr Irene Ilott, an independent occupational therapy consultant.

References

1   Ilott I, Mead J, Roberts J and Hammond R (2004) *Enhancing stakeholder involvement in NICE guideline development: learning lessons from the experience of the allied health professions, health visiting, midwifery and nursing.* Clinical Effectiveness Forum for Allied Health Professions: London.

2   National Institute for Clinical Excellence (2004a) *The guideline development process: an overview for stakeholders, the public and the NHS.* NICE: London.

3   National Institute for Clinical Excellence (2004b) *Guideline development methods: information for National Collaborating Centres and guideline developers.* NICE: London.

For a copy of the full or summary report, please email your details to: The Library and Information Services at the Chartered Society of Physiotherapy. Email: lis@csp.org.uk. Tel: + 44 (0)20 7306 6666.

Developing and implementing NICE guidance

The Health Technology Assessment Programme: supporting NICE

Tom Walley

The HTA Programme aims to identify NHS research needs in relation to new or existing technologies, so that we can provide answers to the key questions at the time decision-makers need them. A health technology is almost anything that the NHS uses or undertakes for potential patient benefit, e.g. a new or old drug, an operation, a way of screening for disease. Decision-makers here are anyone who uses or purchases a technology, or who advises on its use. The HTA programme has now been running for 11 years and its work can be broadly divided into two types of research: primary research – creating new information – and research synthesis, i.e. assembling and interpreting existing information, in the form of systematic reviews, and often with appropriate economic evaluations.

We support the NICE appraisals programme by commissioning this second form of research. To date we have undertaken over 80 assessments on behalf of NICE, ranging from 14 to 18 per year. The technologies to be appraised are decided by the Secretary of State for Health. Each appraisal by NICE has to be supported by a Technology Assessment Report (TAR). These address the clinical evidence behind a technology, and conduct an economic evaluation of the technology. Finally they consider the budgetary consequences of the use of a technology in the NHS. But they do not make recommendations about whether the NHS should use the technology or not – that is the job of the NICE appraisals committees. These committees receive not just the clinical and economic evidence in the TAR, but also submissions from a manufacturer of a new technology or from clinical experts who have experience of it and, perhaps most important of all, from patients who might either benefit from or suffer from the application of this technology. The appraisal committee must take all of these on board and come to a judgement, even where evidence is uncertain (*see* Figure A).

The HTA programme funds and supports seven independent academic teams across the UK to undertake the TARs. They work to a call-off contract and each

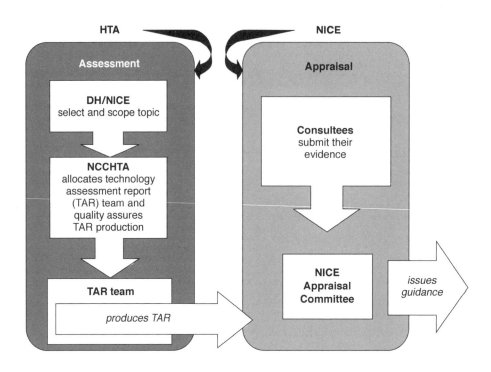

Figure A The HTA programme and NICE appraisals.

delivers between three to six TARs per year. They require key skills in systematic reviewing, often using very limited evidence, and in health economic evaluation and modelling. They must involve clinical experts to help them in their work, often changing with each topic. The teams also attend the appraisal committees to help them interpret the report and identify areas where the evidence is poor – often the case for new technologies. They may undertake further work that the appraisals committee may feel is necessary after its first meeting.

This work is difficult: it is always done to challenging timelines, and depending on the technology under appraisal, may involve systematic reviews embracing over a hundred studies; it requires the assessment of perhaps several manufacturers' submissions, and usually the creation of a new health economic model. Finally the work is presented to the appraisal committee before the team drops the topic and moves on to a totally different project. The nature of the work has developed substantially over the past 4–5 years, as NICE's systems have developed and become more sophisticated, and its information require-ments have increased. The quality of the work has also had to increase to meet more and more rigorous demands from NICE, and it is this quality that has allowed the process of NICE appraisals to be recognised as the international gold standard.

The teams in general are conservative in their approach, being heavily influenced by the philosophy of evidence-based medicine, and perhaps inherently suspicious of the enthusiasm of manufacturers or some clinical experts about new and often unproven technologies. As described above, the appraisals committees have many other influences apart from the TAR. The guidance issued by NICE therefore sometimes is not entirely in accord with the strictly evidence-based assessment report.

A key problem for the teams is disruption to the flow of work due to external matters beyond their and NICE's control, e.g. drugs failing in the licensing process. The teams are academic and must therefore satisfy their universities that the work is not just invaluable to the NHS, but also of sufficient academic rigour to allow them to make good returns in the research assessment exercise. The teams are encouraged to publish their assessment reports in peer-reviewed journals and they are also published as an HTA monograph. Despite the problems, the teams are enthusiastic about the work, which they see as having a direct influence on national policy – a satisfying result for an academic team. From NICE, it is acknowledged that 'the quality of the Institute's appraisals would never have been achieved without the HTA programme' (Sir Michael Rawlins).

However, NICE is more than just appraisals and the HTA programme more than just research synthesis: we also undertake primary research. We are keen to use NICE research recommendations – gaps in the current evidence identified by NICE in its appraisal or guideline or interventional procedures processes – to inform the topics for this research. An example of primary research undertaken on behalf of NICE is an evaluation of photodynamic therapy, the subject of a NICE appraisal in 2003 (No 68). Key questions about the long-term benefits of this treatment remain unanswered. NICE recommended that 'PDT is used in wet age-related macular degeneration only as part of ongoing or new clinical trials that are designed to generate robust and relevant outcome data, including data on quality of life and costs'. But at this point, it was clear that a randomised placebo-controlled trial would not be feasible or possible. The HTA programme has therefore commissioned a longitudinal cohort study to evaluate its long-term effectiveness, collecting the type of data outlined by NICE and comparing it to historical controls. This so far is the only example of a specific study undertaken at the behest of NICE, but we are keen to work with NICE more in the future. We have agreed that we will help NICE to define its research recommendations; NICE will prioritise these and we will take forward the top two or three priorities identified by NICE for further research each year without further consideration. Other important topics selected by NICE will go through the HTA's standard prioritisation programme. This is a new development for both the HTA programme and NICE, and will undoubtedly mature over the coming years.

Undoubtedly there will be new challenges ahead in the methodologies of technology assessment reviews; the HTA programme is enthusiastic about funding and commissioning this work – NICE is for us a key decision-maker and working with NICE helps us to achieve our aim: delivering answers to the right questions at the right time.

Disseminating a psychological treatment for eating disorders

Christopher G Fairburn

Introduction

In January 2004 the National Institute for Clinical Excellence (NICE) published its clinical guidelines on eating disorders.[1] These guidelines included many recommendations regarding the treatment and management of anorexia nervosa, bulimia nervosa and the atypical eating disorders ('eating disorders not otherwise specified'). (See Fairburn and Harrison[2] for a concise account of these disorders.) There was in essence just one strong evidence-based treatment recommendation (a 'level A' recommendation), which was that patients with bulimia nervosa or binge eating disorder (a provisional new diagnosis for those with recurrent binge eating in the absence of extreme weight-control behaviour) should be offered a specific form of CBT.

In this article certain of the challenges posed by this recommendation are considered, the focus being on how to disseminate within the UK National Health Service (NHS) a specific psychological treatment.

Cognitive behaviour therapy for bulimia nervosa and binge eating disorder

The treatment advocated by NICE is a form of psychotherapy. It was developed by the author in the late 1970s[3] and has been the subject of extensive research ever since. Various detailed descriptions of the treatment have been published (e.g., Fairburn, Marcus and Wilson[4]) and it has evolved considerably.[5] The treatment involves 16 to 20 treatment sessions over about 20 weeks and it is provided on a one-to-one basis by a suitably trained therapist. The availability of the treatment within the NHS is not known, either in terms of the extent of its use or the quality of the CBT provided. It is the author's clinical impression that few patients receive it, a state of affairs that is not peculiar to Britain.[6]

In principle the resources required to implement CBT are straightforward. These are a place in which to deliver the treatment (i.e. an appropriately furnished quiet office) and a therapist who has the necessary expertise and sufficient time. And for the NICE recommendation to be implemented as intended, these resources need to be available at convenient (for the patient) locations across England and Wales. The personnel and financial ramifications of the recommendation will not be considered in this article, although they are of obvious importance. Rather, the focus will be on how to train sufficient clinicians to deliver the treatment.

Disseminating a psychological treatment

There is no system in place for disseminating a psychological treatment across the NHS, nor has there been any research on how best to do this. The barriers to such dissemination are formidable (the financial and personnel considerations aside). They include the following:

1 Lack of knowledge among clinicians and managers about those treatments that are evidence-based and cost-effective. To a large extent this lack of knowledge has been addressed by the publication and widespread circulation of the NICE guidelines together with the pressure to implement its recommendations.
2 A paucity of clinicians with the relevant expertise. Few clinicians in the UK have been trained to deliver this form of CBT.
3 Inertia in the healthcare delivery system. This is a well-recognised problem and one that is not peculiar to the implementation of changes in psychiatric practice.
4 Active resistance to learning and practising new psychological treatments. Some therapists are heavily invested in their old ways of working and are reluctant to change.

In the absence of research on the best way to train therapists to deliver CBT, it is the author's view that a reasonable model to follow is that used in the major clinical research trials (e.g. Agras *et al.*[7]). This involves two steps. First, suitably qualified clinicians attend an introductory 'workshop' in which a detailed description of the treatment is provided. In the case of this form of CBT such a workshop typically lasts two days. Then the trainees are provided with ongoing clinical supervision. The professional background of the trainees is less important than having some experience helping patients with eating disorders and being willing and able to deliver a short-term psychological treatment designed to produce behaviour change. Professional groups with potentially relevant experience include clinical psychologists, psychiatrists, nurses, dieticians, social workers and occupational therapists.

  Translating this model to the dissemination of CBT across the NHS requires encouraging suitable clinicians to attend a two-day workshop and providing subsequent ongoing clinical supervision. With regard to the workshop, it is clearly essential that the presenter is an expert in CBT and preferably someone with a high profile (to attract clinicians to attend). The workshop needs to have as its goal the engendering of enthusiasm among potential therapists and the provision of a thorough description of the treatment. It needs to be interactive and include salient clinical examples and the demonstration of important distinctive procedures. It also needs to be accompanied by the provision of detailed written supporting material.

Progress to date

The author has attempted to take on this challenge. To date he has conducted five national two-day workshops as well as four regional ones. Over 1000 clinicians have attended. He has also developed a way of providing ongoing supervision for interested clinical teams (via videoconferencing). At present three teams are being supervised, with further teams being supervised soon. The goal is that in addition to learning how to deliver the treatment, these teams also acquire the expertise needed to train and supervise others.

Acknowledgements

CGF is supported by a Principal Research Fellowship from the Wellcome Trust (046386).

References

1   National Collaborating Centre for Mental Health (2004) *Eating Disorders: Core Interventions in the Treatment and Management of Anorexia Nervosa, Bulimia Nervosa and Related Eating Disorders.* British Psychological Society and Royal College of Psychiatrists: London. www.nice.org.uk.

2   Fairburn CG and Harrison PJ (2003) Eating disorders. *The Lancet* **61**: 407–16.

3   Fairburn CG (1981) A cognitive behavioural approach to the treatment of bulimia. *Psychological Medicine* **11**: 707–11.

4   Fairburn CG, Marcus MD and Wilson GT (1993) Cognitive-behavioral therapy for binge eating and bulimia nervosa: A comprehensive treatment manual. In: CG Fairburn and GT Wilson (eds). *Binge eating: nature, assessment and treatment.* Guilford Press: New York, pp 361–404.

5   Fairburn CG, Cooper Z and Shafran R (2003) Cognitive behaviour therapy for eating disorders: A 'transdiagnostic' theory and treatment. *Behaviour Research and Therapy* **41**: 509–28.

6   Crow S, Mussell MP, Peterson C, Knopke A and Mitchell J (1999) Prior treatment received by patients with bulimia nervosa. *International Journal of Eating Disorders* **25**: 39–44.

7   Agras WS, Walsh BT, Fairburn CG, Wilson GT and Kraemer HC (2000) A multicenter comparison of cognitive-behavioral therapy and interpersonal psychotherapy for bulimia nervosa. *Archives of General Psychiatry* **57**: 459–66.

Improvement Partnership for Ambulance Services: what we do and how we do it

Julia RA Taylor

Context

The Health Minister, Rosie Winterton, announced the launch of IPAS (Improvement Partnership for Ambulance Services) on 23 September 2003. The Programme Director was appointed on 1 November 2003.

IPAS was designed to be a joint venture between the DH and the NHS Modernisation Agency (MA) with the aim of helping ambulance staff to modernise the service and improve the patient experience. The partnership was allocated funding of £1 million and it was anticipated that the programme would cease by December 2004 (this was subsequently extended to March 2005).

The Service Level Agreement with the DH was measured by the following objectives:

- availability of leadership development options to all Ambulance Trusts with positive feedback from course participants
- improved star ratings for the 2002/03 0- and 1-star trusts: in the 2004/05 performance ratings three out of the nine 1-star trusts will have an improved star rating for 2004/05 performance ratings
- two Learning Exchange events to be held in November 2003
- development of a fully functioning Modernisation Agency (MA) IPAS website
- development of specific learning material for Ambulance Trusts
- development of good practice checklist for Ambulance Trusts.

All objectives were met by September 2004, ahead of schedule.

The IPAS model of work

As IPAS had limited human (a maximum of three whole time equivalents (WTE)) and financial resources, and was expected to deliver in a relatively short space of time, IPAS adopted a key principle of collaborative working to deliver the work streams.

The IPAS Steering Board, consisting of a broad cross-section of influential stakeholders, was set up. Membership included representatives from the DH Ambulance Policy Team, MA, Ambulance Trust Chief Executives and the Healthcare Commission. These volunteers were able to guide IPAS as to individuals or teams with the appropriate experience and expertise required by IPAS to further its activities or networks.

Through this guiding principle, the following key methods of delivery were adopted:

- engaging key stakeholders with the required knowledge, expertise or experience
- utilising existing networks
- asking for assistance to fill knowledge/expertise gaps, i.e. by approaching Trusts, Workforce Development Confederations (WDCs), SHAs, Modernisation Agency teams
- using different methods to gain expertise/contributions, i.e. focus groups for individual activities/events, interviews, documentation, etc.
- taking the responsibility for leading and delivering activities/events
- commissioning activities to fill the gaps that collaborative working cannot meet
- utilising free accommodation from Trusts and other organisations to hold training and events.

The next phase was using this key principle to deliver the four main work streams. These were:

- a Leadership Development Portfolio specifically targeted towards the learning and development needs of Ambulance Trust staff (with funding support for the challenged organisations)
- Performance Improvement Networks to develop communities of practice
- 'Good Practice Guidelines' around issues that Ambulance Trusts were struggling with
- IPAS Affiliates to support challenged Trusts.

1   **Leadership Development Portfolio:** Speed was of an essence, so initially we looked to see what was available which we could support access into for the Ambulance Trusts.

We used the existing Leadership Centre portfolio, selecting elements pertinent to the Ambulance Trusts' needs, then funding places. Some elements of the Leadership Centre portfolio were specifically redirected to Ambulance Trusts through negotiation with Leadership Centre Directors, as the focus on Ambulance Trusts had not been present before.

A programme to plug a significant gap identified was filled by tendering and commissioning a supplier to deliver a national senior and middle management development programme (the IPAS SaM), specifically designed

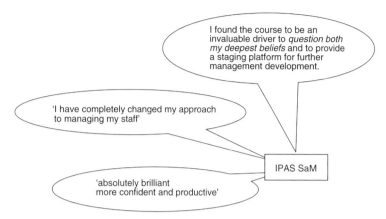

I found the course to be an invaluable driver to *question both my deepest beliefs* and to provide a staging platform for further management development.

'I have completely changed my approach to managing my staff'

IPAS SaM

'absolutely brilliant more confident and productive'

Figure A IPAS SaM

for Ambulance Trusts. Ambulance Trust staff were consulted regarding the design and it was delivered to 14 of the 31 Ambulance Trusts and to nearly 200 staff.

A development programme for Ambulance Medical Directors was designed and delivered by IPAS with support from the Leadership Centre.

2 **Spread and dissemination of good practice:** Three 'Good Practice Guidelines' have been developed:

- *Best Practice Guidelines on Ambulance Operations Management*
- *Human Resource Guidelines for Ambulance Services* – to assist in the delivery and measurement of your HR Services from IWL (improving working lives) to CNST (Clinical Negligence Scheme for Trusts)
- *'Driving Change' Good Practice Guidelines for PCTs on Commissioning Arrangements for Emergency Ambulance Services and Non-Emergency Patient Transport Services* – this document was launched at an event for PCTs with their Ambulance Trusts to support their comprehension of how improved commissioning of Ambulance Trusts can assist the whole health economy.

3 **Developing communities of practice:** Three have been set up:

- Directors of Operations: four regional sets supported by professional facilitators, for 12 months with an action plan to be self-sustainable subsequently. Outcomes are improved working together and learning, e.g. when Greater Manchester Ambulance Service responded to change in the Cat C Performance Requirement, they wrote: 'Greater Manchester Ambulance Service proposal outlines incremental changes in the management of Category C incidents, including changes in the performance standard. The approach has been developed in conjunction with neighbouring Ambulance Trusts Lancashire, Mersey and West Yorkshire as part of the IPAS northern group.'
- Clinical Governance Leads: four regional sets supported by an MA

facilitator for six months with an action plan to be self-sustainable subsequently.

- Patient and Public Involvement Leads: Pump primed by a one-day event to share good practice in the morning with the afternoon facilitated to help; then initiate local communities of practice.
  - 'Very worthwhile, just sorry that agency won't be around to run another day like this.'
  - 'Thanks for organising the event, and giving us a nudge to take more action in future.'
  - What were the high spots? 'Networking. Not feeling alone. Being comforted by sharing views and ideas – knowing we are all going in the same direction.'
  - 'Networking, sharing information. Well set up.'
  - 'Hearing how other services operate, learning about PALS (Patient Advice and Liaison Service) and making new contacts.'

4 IPAS Affiliates
- IPAS Affiliates (expert volunteers) to support challenged trusts: The original proposal was to second staff from Ambulance Trusts; however, due to the shortfall in capacity in Ambulance Trusts this was not a viable option. IPAS Affiliates have also provided valuable expertise, access to their networks and delivery of some of the IPAS work streams. Examples of support include:
  - One Trust needed a wide range of support from achieving key targets to handling human resource issues. We also brokered local relationships.
  - Another requested support on Major Incident Planning, demand and capacity, clinical governance and clinical effectiveness.
  - We are often requested to provide support regarding refining their control room.
  - Some Trusts or SHA have requested support on commissioning models.

Implementing pressure ulcer guidance: a success story

Menna Lloyd-Jones and Trudie Young

Introduction

In April 2001 the National Institute for Clinical Excellence (NICE) released Clinical Guideline B *Pressure Ulcer Risk Assessment and Prevention*.[1] These were inherited from the Royal College of Nursing Clinical Practice Guidelines on pressure ulcer risk assessment and prevention.[2] However, these guidelines were incomplete since they required further information relating to pressure-relieving equipment. Consequently the NICE formed a guideline development group to review the literature and to address the outstanding issue. The final document entitled *Pressure ulcer risk assessment and prevention, including the use of pressure-relieving devices (beds, mattresses and overlays) for the prevention of pressure ulcers in primary and secondary care. Clinical Guideline 7* was published in October 2003.[3] Although NICE develops and disseminates guidance, they have no formal responsibility for implementation.[4] This paper describes how a partnership between the North West Wales National Health Service Trust and the University of Wales, Bangor has worked to produce a successful guideline implementation strategy.

Guideline implementation

It should be noted that NICE acknowledges[4] that their guidance is not isolated from the challenges and barriers to implementation. They suggest that implementation can be enhanced by working in partnerships. As a result the Tissue Viability Teams within the three National Health Service Trusts, in North Wales, have worked together to ensure uniformity of approach when adapting and implementing the national guidelines for local use. The teams utilised the NICE Guidelines to inform clinical practice and to direct clinical decision-making, in order to improve patient outcomes with regard to pressure ulcer prevention and management.

Grimshaw *et al.*[5] suggest there is an imperfect evidence base to support guideline dissemination and implementation strategies. Consequently the local implementation strategy became a dynamic process that started with the publication of the guideline (*see* Table A). The initial dissemination strategies involved raising awareness at a local tissue viability conference as well as at link nurse meetings. However, the implementation cannot be expected to

Table A North Wales guideline implementation process

Implementation process	Action	Rationale
National Institute for Clinical Excellence Guidelines published	Local adaptation of guideline and development of audit tool	Uniformity of approach across North Wales
Dissemination	Launch of guidelines at local tissue viability conference and link nurse meetings	Raise local awareness
Educational initiative	Development of self-directed teaching packs for qualified and unqualified nurses	Provide detail of the guideline content to nurses and healthcare assistants
Continuing professional development programme	Integrated the guideline content into the tissue viability diploma and degree modules for trained nurses	Inform the nursing staff of the guideline content and the underpinning evidence
Audit	Biannual retrospective audit of patient records using adapted Royal College of Nursing audit tool	Evaluate the extent of compliance at individual ward level
Audit-related practice developments	Development of repositioning schedule	Strengthen nursing documentation and assist in audit process
	Development of seating assessment	Ensure multi-professional contribution to implementation
Audit-related educational developments	Healthcare assistant competency framework	Safe clinical practice
	CD-ROM	Educational material in a multiprofessional user format

produce clinical changes by solely raising awareness. As suggested by NICE,[4] incorporating guidance into continuing professional development programmes will further encourage its use in clinical practice. As a consequence educational material was developed to support guideline implementation. The educational initiatives included the development of guideline specific self-directed teaching packs as well as a CD-ROM. The materials did not require attendance at study days because this was felt to be necessary in an environment where the pressures for mandatory training are already having a significant impact on ward staffing levels. The initial target audience for these materials was nursing staff, but they are now being used by various healthcare professionals involved in pressure ulcer prevention and management (e.g. those who attend Trust induction programmes and healthcare assistants). It should be noted that the latter have a competency framework to ensure safe clinical practice.

Twelve months after the initial implementation, an audit was undertaken using the adapted Royal College of Nursing tool.[6] The audit highlighted significant gaps in compliance within the guideline. Examples included an inability to record timings of pressure ulcer risk assessment (this is a result of there being no space for this detail on the current documentation), repositioning charts were also not in use and seating assessments were not being carried out. The implementation process is still being refined and the input of other healthcare professionals is feeding into the process. For example, occupational therapists are now working with the Tissue Viability Nurse to provide advice on seating assessments and equipment purchase.

Conclusion

Guideline implementation has to be a dynamic process that incorporates an audit cycle. Clinical issues often only arise once the guidelines become active, and organisations should therefore have the flexibility to respond to any clinical barriers to guideline implementation. A variety of strategies are required to raise awareness, provide educational support, and permeate the guideline content to all relevant healthcare professionals. Partnerships allow for the exchange of ideas across professions, and ultimately improve patient outcomes through the application of best practice initiatives.

However, within pressure ulcer prevention and management, it should be noted that treatment-based targets, quality indicators of care and subsequent rating systems have to be viewed with caution so as to ensure the outcome measures accurately assess the impact of guidelines in clinical practice.

References

1   National Institute for Clinical Excellence (2001) *Pressure Ulcer Risk Management and Prevention. Inherited clinical guideline B*. National Institute for Clinical Excellence: London.

3   National Institute for Clinical Excellence (2003) *Pressure ulcer risk assessment and preven-tion, including the use of pressure-relieving devices (beds, mattresses and overlays) for the prevention of pressure ulcers in primary and secondary care. Clinical Guideline 7*. National Institute for Clinical Excellence: London.

2   Royal College of Nursing (2001) *Pressure Ulcer Risk Assessment and Prevention*. Royal College of Nursing: London.

4   National Institute for Clinical Excellence (2004) *Supporting the Implementation of NICE Guidance*. National Institute for Clinical Excellence: London. www.nice.org.uk

5   Grimshaw JM, Thomas RE, MacLennan G, Fraser C, Ramsay CR, Vale L *et al.* (2004) Effectiveness and efficiency of guideline dissemination and implementation strategies. *Health Technology Assessment* **8**: 66.

6   Royal College of Nursing (2003) *Pressure Ulcer Risk Assessment and Prevention implemen-tation guide and audit protocol*. Royal College of Nursing: London.

Implementing head injury guidance

A David Mendelow

Head injuries are common (2000 per 100 000 per year) and less than 2% are treated in the 30 neurosurgery units in England. There is Class 2 evidence that delay of as little as 2 hours in the surgical evacuation of acute subdural[1] and extradural[2] haematomas is associated with poor outcome. The initial triage of those patients that require urgent surgery is therefore critical to their management. Guidelines for their triage have been in use for 20 years in various forms (Society of British Neurosurgeons,[3] Royal College of Surgeons, Scottish Intercollegiate Guideline Network). These were based on clinical risk factors and the presence of skull fracture on skull X-ray (SXR).[4] The disadvantage of this was that SXR does not have 100% sensitivity and specificity for a haematoma. By contrast, CT scanning will accurately identify all surgically significant haematomas.

The NICE guidelines for the initial triage of head-injured patients recommend that the primary imaging should be with the CT scan and the SXR is restricted to young children at risk of intracranial injury and, in conjunction with high-quality observation, to situations where CT scanning is not available. The NICE guidelines specify a tight timescale of 1 hour for obtaining the CT scan. They are based on Class I evidence from the Canadian CT Head Rule (Stiell *et al.*[5]). The 5-point CT Head Rule has 100% specificity for surgical intervention, while the 7-point rule has 98% specificity for any intracranial abnormality. The former requires that 32% of all head-injured patients are scanned, while the 7-point rule requires that 54% are scanned. From the surgical viewpoint the 5-point rule is the urgent one and the 7-point rule is really not at all urgent unless there is clinical deterioration. The Canadian CT Head Rule has now been explicitly and prospectively re-evaluated in a separate cohort of head-injured patients,[5] thus adding to its strength as Class I evidence.

Implementation of these NICE guidelines is difficult and complex because in most English hospitals there would be an increase in the demand for urgent CT scanning. This would be variable because some hospitals have tried to implement the ATLS (advanced trauma life support) recommendations from the American College of Surgeons: these result in nearly all head-injured patients requiring a CT and thus the NICE guidelines could lead to a reduction in the CT scan rate!

To evaluate the impact of implementation of these NICE guidelines on the CT scan, SXR and admission rates we have prospectively evaluated a specific and detailed implementation plan in the Emergency Department (ED) at one peripheral major District General Hospital (North Tyneside General Hospital = NTGH) and compared with the EDs of two other hospitals, each associated with a Regional Neurosurgical Unit (Newcastle General Hospital = NGH and Hope Hospital in Manchester = HH).

The results have indicated that, when full implementation was very actively pursued at NTGH, the CT rate increased eightfold, while SXRs were virtually eliminated (*see* Table A) and admissions were not in fact reduced. By contrast at the two other hospitals, where no such deliberate implementation policy took place, the CT scan rate only doubled with varying effects on SXR and admission rates.

Table A Attendance rates in A&E, CT and SXR rates and admissions before and after the introduction of the NICE head injury guidelines at three different hospitals

	NTGH before	*NTGH after*	*NGH before*	*NGH after*	*HH before*	*HH after*
Head injury attendances	245	351	257	291	221	282
CT scans	4	33	17	24	7	20
SXRs	52	2	59	80	81	11
Admissions	17	27	39	30	21	11

NTGH = North Tyneside General Hospital; NGH = Newcastle General Hospital; HH = Hope Hospital (Manchester)

Similar findings have now been reported from Cambridge[6] and Leeds,[7] where the CT rate was also estimated to rise between two- and fourfold.

From these various sources it can be estimated that the increase in CT scans needed to implement the NICE guidelines would be between two- and eightfold, depending on which guidelines had been in place previously. All these reports have confirmed that the reduction in SXRs more than offsets the costs of the CT scans. However, the training and overtime payments for the radiographers who are needed to carry out the scans should not be underestimated – indeed, this would appear to be the main problem with implementation. Also, the predicted reduction in the number of admissions did not take place, so that some of the economic factors may have to be revised.

Pilot studies in the Northern Region have led to the following pragmatic interpretation of the NICE head injury guidelines:

- GCS < 13 at any point since the injury should be documented by a nurse, doctor or paramedic.
- Senior guidance should be sought in the case of children.
- The 5-point rule should be invoked for urgent CT scans; the 7-point rule would point to the need for scanning in normal working hours, unless there is deterioration during the observation period.
- For patients over 65 years of age who remain fully conscious (GCS = 15) CT scanning can also be deferred until normal working hours unless there is deterioration during the observation period.

Implementation of the NICE guidelines for the triage of head-injured patients should eliminate delays in the surgical evacuation of haematomas, reduce the use of SXRs and identify brain damage on CT that is not necessarily surgical. This identification may help with rehabilitation needs. Only a national audit would truly reflect the impact of these guidelines on these numbers and this would have to be started now if a true 'before and after' effect is to be demonstrated. It may already be too late because implementation has been introduced haphazardly: the data presented here may therefore be the only prospectively collected data that will ever be available from the pre-NICE guideline era.

References

1 Seelig JM, Becker DP, Miller JD, Greenberg RP, Ward JD and Choi SC (1981) Traumatic acute subdural hematoma: major mortality reduction in comatose patients treated within four hours. *New England Journal of Medicine* **305**: 1511–18.

2 Mendelow AD, Karmi MZ, Paul KS, Fuller GA and Gillingham FJ (1979) Extradural haematoma – effect of delayed treatment. *BMJ* **1**: 1240–1242.

3 Bartlett J, Kett-White R, Mendelow AD, Miller JD, Pickard J and Teasdale GM (1998) Guidelines for the initial management of head injuries. Recommendations from the Society of British Neurological Surgeons (Members of the Working Party of the Society of British Neurological Surgeons). *British Journal of Neurosurgery* **12**: 349–52.

4 Teasdale GM, Murray G, Anderson E *et al.* (1990) Risks of acute traumatic intracranial haematoma in children and adults: implications for the management of head injuries. *BMJ* **300**: 363–7.

5 Stiell IG, Wells GA, Vandemheen K *et al.* (2001) The Canadian CT Head Rule for patients with minor head injury. *The Lancet* **357**: 1391–6.

6 Sultan HY, Boyle A, Pereira M, Antonu N and Maimari C (2004) Application of the Canadian CT Head Rules in managing minor head injuries in a UK Emergency Department: Implications for the implementation of the NICE guidelines. *Emergency Medicine Journal* **21**: 420–5.

7 Miller L, Kent RM and Tennant A (2004) Audit of head injury management in Accident and Emergency at two hospitals: implications for NICE CT guidelines. *BMC Health Services Research* **4**: 7. www.biomedcentral.com/1472-6963/4/7

Implementation of NICE guidance: an ABPI perspective

David Brickwood

This study used IMS sales to track changes (in some cases) in several therapeutic classes pre and post the publication of NICE Guidance, as well as looking at the occurrence of regional variations of prescribing practice by strategic health authorities. The data does not take into account specific prescribing practices or individual patient data and it was not subjected to any statistical analysis. Interpretation of the data is based on subjective visual tracking of the data curves only.

Several therapeutic areas were studied and the following broad conclusions can be drawn.

1   Where initiation of therapy is predominantly conducted in the primary care setting it is difficult to draw any conclusions that the publication of a positive recommendation to prescribe a particular class of products is having any significant effect. This is exemplified by the class of the glitazone therapies for the treatment of diabetes. (see Figure A) Three pieces of guidance have been issued by NICE for this class of medicines as indicated by the thick vertical lines, in August 2000, March 2001 and August 2003.

2   Some impact of NICE can be seen where products have been initiated in secondary care but managed in the primary care arena. This is exemplified by the case of the acetylcholinesterase inhibitors for the treatment of mild to moderate Alzheimer's disease (see Figure B). A positive recommendation for the class was issued in January 2001, as indicated by the thick vertical line. The horizontal line shows an estimate of the level of uptake of this guidance, which has clearly been exceeded in practice. However, the difference in prescribing patterns between the lowest adopting strategic health authorities and the highest has become more pronounced after the publication of a positive recommendation for the class (see Figure C).

3   There are some cases where products are used predominantly in the secondary care arena where a positive NICE recommendation has an impact on prescribing behaviour, for example in the case of the glycoprotein IIb/III inhibitors for the treatment of acute coronary syndromes (see Figure D). The

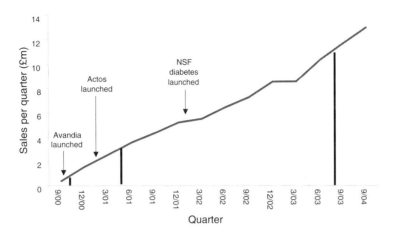

Figure A Glitazones.

first piece of guidance was issued in September 2000 and replaced in 2002, again indicated by the two vertical lines.

In conclusion, the issues behind implementation of NICE guidance are multifactorial and complex and there is no magic bullet to solve this problem. The availability of budget and human resources to track and implement changes appears to be a major factor. Planning for these changes seems highly variable. Also, in

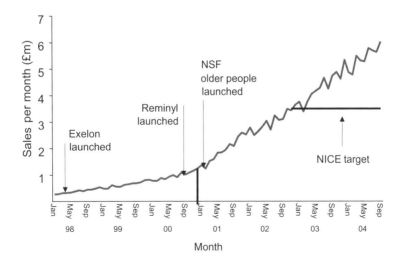

Figure B Alzheimer's disease.

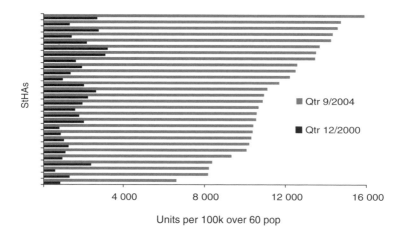

Figure C Alzheimer's disease.

a sense there is a need for unifying team agenda at a local level, together with a measurement toolkit for tracking progress. Audit, monitoring and the establishment of incentives to change prescribing behaviour are suggested key success factors in driving change.

The pharmaceutical industry has a role to play in helping this process, as there are opportunities to share product, customer and market knowledge with

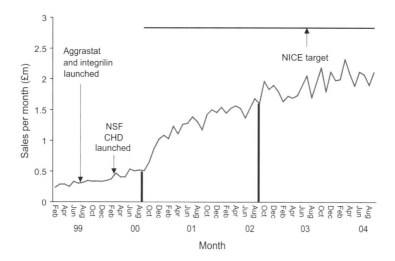

Figure D Glycoprotein IIB/III inhibitors.

prescribers. Also, the industry could help in sharing best practice and offering project management skills in implementation planning.

The recent appointment of an Implementation Systems Director at NICE is an important step along the way but engagement of the Healthcare Commission in placing the implementation of NICE guidance at the top of the agenda is believed to be a critical factor for long-term success.

Acknowledgements

Thanks to Jane Poyntz at Policy Matters and Phil O'Neil at the ABPI for their valuable contributions towards this article.

Measuring the impact of NICE guidance across 28 disease areas

Simon Howard

Introduction

If clinicians were adopting NICE recommendations, one would expect to see a change in clinical practice in line with the recommendations. In December 2003, NICE commissioned Abacus to measure the impact of 28 individual pieces of NICE guidance. This paper summarises the results presented at the NICE conference in December 2004. The full report is available through the NICE website.

Aims and objectives

To measure the impact of NICE guidance across 28 selected disease areas.

Methodology

IMS provided data specific for England and Wales for 20 of the topics under review.

Datasets included

1 Disease Analyser: Primary care prescribing (patients/prescriptions).
2 British Pharmaceutical Index (BPI): Primary care product usage (units).
3 Hospital Pharmacy Audit (HPA): Hospital product usage (units).
4 Oncology Database: Cancer (patients).

Where no IMS data was available, individual manufacturers unit sales data were combined to provide a total picture for England and Wales. For obesity surgery, specialist centres were contacted directly and numbers of obesity procedures performed before and after guidance publication was audited.

Results were presented as moving annual totals (MATs) to give a global trend analysis pre- and post-guidance publication.

Results

In this analysis of 28 of the earlier NICE reviews there were 33 different recommendations. Approximately one-third of these recommendations were for first-line or routine product use and 57% were a recommendation for second/third-line use or for a defined patient risk group. Only four sets of guidance could be classified as negative.

Surgery for morbid obesity

In July 2002 NICE recommended the use of gastric bands and surgical treatments for the morbidly obese.

This audit of the major suppliers of gastric bands and the prime centres for obesity surgery shows a significant increase in sales and use of bands in the

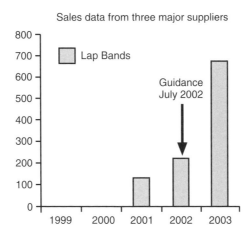

NICE estimates suggest target of 500 procedures in year 1 growing to 4000 procedures over 8 years

Figure A Unit sales of gastric bands in England and Wales.

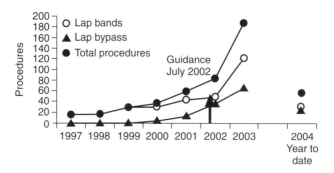

64% procedures in 2003 used lap band (58% in 2002)

Figure B Obesity surgery procedures reported in 7 of 12 Trusts. Lap band versus lap bypass surgery for obesity.

year following guidance. There were in the region of 700 surgical procedures carried out in 2003, in line with year 1 expectations described in the NICE guidance.

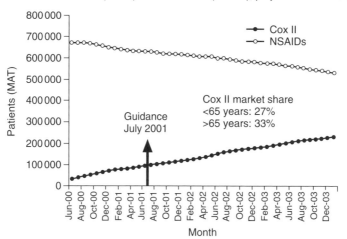

Figure C Cox II versus NSAID prescribing.

Cox II prescribing for arthritis

Cox II agents were recommended in preference to NSAIDs for 'at risk' arthritis patients. There has been no significant change in the gradual trend from NSAIDs to Cox II agents, suggesting that guidance was endorsing standard practice.

Riluzole for motor neurone disease

Riluzole was recommended for the treatment of motor neurone disease (MND) in NICE guidance published in January 2001. There are an estimated 2000 patients with MND in England and Wales.

In secondary care, the growth rate of riluzole did not change following guidance publication. In primary care, the effect of NICE guidance was to accelerate the use of riluzole, adding about 4000 units per year. Approximately 70% of the total potential patient group now receive riluzole.

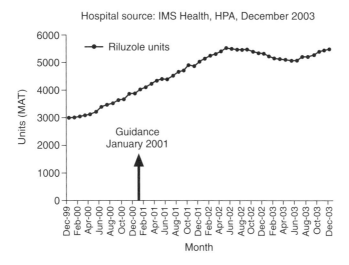

Riluzole was recommended for the treatment of MND (estimated 2000 patients)
2000 patients would consume a maximum of 26 000 units (13, 28 day units)

Figure D Units of riluzole dispensed in hospital pharmacy.

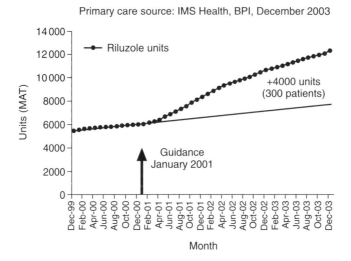

Primary care source: IMS Health, BPI, December 2003

Riluzole was recommended for the treatment of MND (estimated 2000 patients)
2000 patients would consume a maximum 26 000 units (13, 28 day units)

Figure E Units of riluzole dispensed in retail pharmacy.

Oxaliplatin, irinotecan and raltitrexed for advanced colorectal cancer

The guidance reviewing oxaliplatin, irinotecan and raltitrexed for use in advanced colorectal cancer gave three separate recommendations (first-line, second-line and not recommended, respectively).

IMS data shows an increase in prescribing of oxaliplatin as a first-choice therapy, irinotecan as second-line therapy and an absence of raltitrexed prescribing.

This disease area is a very good example of how NICE recommendations can shape prescribing behaviour.

Topotecan and PLDH for advanced ovarian cancer

Both topotecan and pegylated liposomal doxorubicin hydrochloride (PLDH) were recommended as second-line treatment options in advanced ovarian cancer after platinum therapy has failed. Between 1500 and 2000 patients are estimated to be suitable for either product. IMS oncology data suggests that 100–150 patients received topotecan and 50–100 patients received PLDH in 2003.

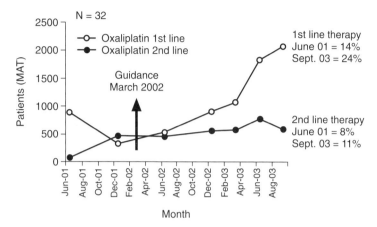

Source: IMS Health, IMS Oncology Database, August 2003

Recommended 1st line in advanced colorectal cancer with resectable liver metastases
NICE based estimate = 3254 patients
IMS projection = 2057 patients 1st line + 579 patients 2nd line

Figure F   Oxaliplatin use in patients with advanced colorectal cancer.

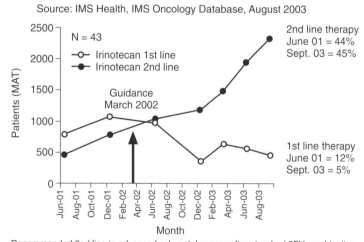

Source: IMS Health, IMS Oncology Database, August 2003

Recommended 2nd line in advanced colorectal cancer after standard 5FU combination
has failed. Potential 12 000 patients based upon NICE estimates
(29 000*55% advanced*75% 2nd line)
IMS projections = 2314 patients 2nd line + 450 patients 1st line

Figure G Irinotecan use in patients with advanced colorectal cancer.

The numbers here are very small and based upon 23 patient records only, therefore caution has to be made when looking at projections. However, it does appear that a 10-fold increase in product use would occur if guidance were to be fully implemented.

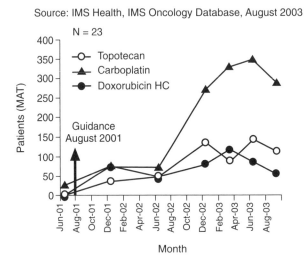

Consider Topotecan or PLDH 2nd line after platinum failure
NICE guidance estimates 1500–2000 patients suitable for either 2nd line option
IMS projections suggest: 100–150 patients on Topotecan, 50–100 patients on PLDH

Figure H Second-line treatments in advanced ovarian cancer.

Beta interferon for multiple sclerosis

Beta interferon was not recommended for use in multiple sclerosis and therefore a decline in units dispensed in hospital would be expected following the publication of guidance. Product growth has been driven by a risk-sharing scheme rather than by NICE guidance.

Growth hormone

Somatropin was recommended for four different types of growth-related diseases. This very positive guidance has turned a product decline into steep growth.

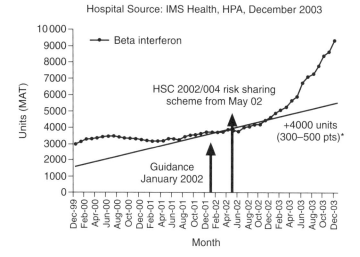

Figure I Beta interferon units dispensed in hospital pharmacy.

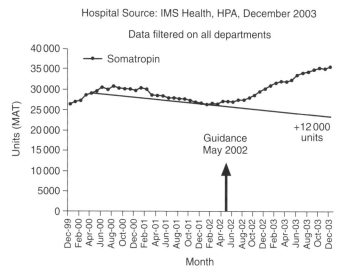

Figure J Hospital use of growth hormone.

Summary and conclusions

This research took a global look at the impact that NICE guidance has had on 28 different disease areas. The methodology used does not give as much detailed information as a prospective audit and should be interpreted as such. We present trends rather than specifics. However some broad conclusions can be drawn.

Of the 28 disease areas reviewed, a third of the recommendations suggested broad or first-line usage. Only four were negative.

There is a broad perception that NICE guidance is not implemented fully enough and certainly not within the required three months following publication. This research suggests that different disease areas have been implemented to varying extents.

There are examples of guidance endorsing current practice resulting in continued product growth but at the same rate as before publication of guidance. Cox IIs and atypical antipsychotics are good examples.

There are examples of accelerated product uptake such as riluzole for motor neurone disease and gastric bands for obesity surgery.

NICE guidance can also influence prescribing pathways, for example driving treatment patterns in colorectal cancer.

NICE guidance is driving change but at different rates for different disease areas. Of the 28 topics we reviewed, 12 could be classed as reasonably implemented within the expectations of guidance. Another 12 were classified as under-implemented and only four were driving utilisation of product above the expectations described in NICE guidance.

Audit into the implementation of NICE guidance for Roche drugs

Paul Catchpole

In order to support the effective implementation of NICE guidance, good monitoring systems must be developed by the NHS to allow tracking of the uptake of guidance at all relevant organisational levels such as GP practices, NHS Trusts, PCTs, SHAs and managed clinical networks such as Cancer Networks. Within primary care, national NHS systems already exist which could be utilised to allow such monitoring to take place, but within secondary care it is more difficult to obtain appropriate prescribing data. Many Roche specialist drugs are sold directly to hospitals and therefore Roche has access to accurate, timely and comprehensive sales data which we utilised to undertake a series of quarterly audits on a selection of the products which have been appraised by NICE.

The methodologies which were developed to do this were first shared with the DH and the Institute in order to obtain feedback on the assumptions. Due to the current absence of appropriate and robust monitoring systems within the NHS, we were encouraged to pursue the audits and share the results obtained.

The audits track the number of eligible patients being prescribed a particular drug against the total eligible population for a locality (calculated according to NICE guidance) over six-month periods. A standard algorithm was used for each audit and is shown below in Box A.

The audit methodologies use regularly updated assumptions based on the best available referenced data sources. We utilise national estimates for prevalence and incidence and no adjustments have been made for cross-boundary flows of patients. It was also not possible to separately identify and remove private patients receiving drugs in NHS hospitals and for some audits, particularly rituximab, it was difficult to estimate off-license and off-label usage. These limitations are set out below in Box B.

Box A Methodology and assumptions

Audits present data on patient uptake based on a comparison of:
- potential eligible patient population calculated from:

  - overall population of locality
  - incidence of disease
  - qualifying patient sub-population, e.g. HER-2 status or 'as per licence'
  - patients fit for/choosing treatment

compared against
- 'actual sales' by locality (e.g. Cancer Network) converted into 'numbers of patients receiving treatment'.

Box B Considerations

- Assumptions are based on best available referenced data sources, supplemented by market research studies where necessary.
- Direct hospital sales utilised but sales for non-Roche drugs based on external data sources (hepatitis and obesity, > 92% coverage).
- Private patients treated in NHS facilities not excluded from audit results (all audits).
- Local geographical variations in incidence/prevalence not reflected (e.g. cancer audits).
- No adjustment for cross boundary patient flows (e.g. hepatitis and cancer audits).
- 'Off-label' and 'off-licence' usage difficult to measure (particularly non-Hodgkin's lymphoma).

NICE guidance for trastuzumab (Herceptin) was issued in March 2002 and since that time many more eligible women with metastatic breast cancer now receive this product (*see* Figure A). However, more than two and a half years after the guidance was issued, in under one-third of cancer networks less than one in two eligible women are receiving it.

NICE guidance for capecitabine (Xeloda) was issued in May 2003 for patients with advanced colorectal and breast cancer to provide a choice for patients to take an oral therapy with equivalent efficacy to an already available IV drug regimen. This guidance provided cancer units with the ability to make significant savings in nurse and pharmacy time and to reduce outpatient attendances since the drug can be taken at home. Separate research undertaken by the

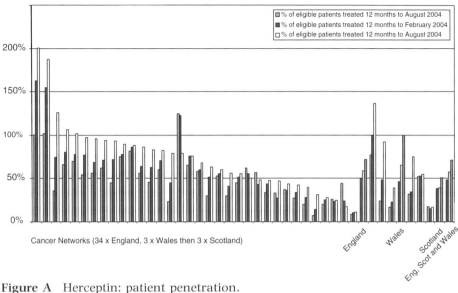

Figure A   Herceptin: patient penetration.

patient charity Colon Cancer Concern showed that, when offered a choice, eight out of ten patients would choose the new oral treatment option. One and a half years after the guidance was issued, uptake still varies considerably across cancer networks with an overall uptake across the UK of around 40% of all eligible patients (*see* Figure B).

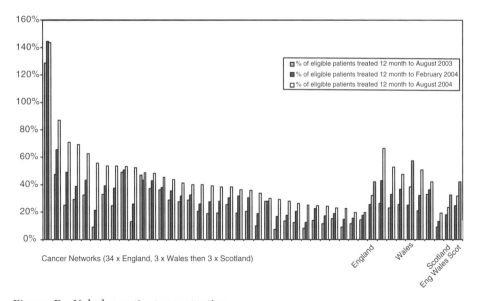

Figure B   Xeloda: patient penetration.

NICE guidance for rituximab (MabThera) was issued in March 2002 and September 2003 for two indications in non-Hodgkin's lymphoma (NHL). Since the respective guidance was issued, two and half years and one year ago, a majority of NHL patients are now being treated with rituximab, although in around one-third of Cancer Networks not all eligible patients are receiving therapy (*see* Figure C). However, the results of this audit need to be qualified because rituximab is also used outside its licensed indications in other haematological malignancies and is also now being used for the treatment of rheumatoid arthritis in some centres. NICE guidance involving drugs which are used in multiple indications are therefore particularly difficult to track accurately and this will need to be taken into account by the NHS when it develops its own NICE guidance tracking systems.

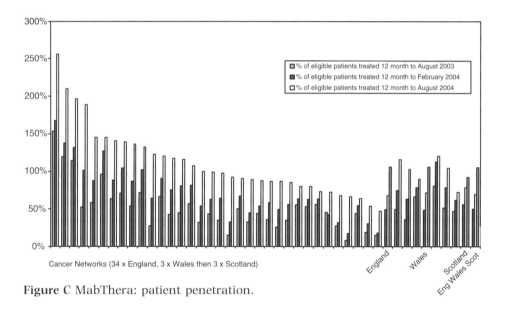

Figure C MabThera: patient penetration.

NICE guidance for obesity drugs was issued in March 2001 and October 2001 respectively for orlistat (Xenical) and sibutramine (Reductil®). Since the guidance was issued three and half and three years ago respectively, many eligible patients are not being offered obesity pharmacotherapy (with eligible patients calculated exactly as in the NICE guidance and according to the criteria set out in the Summary of Product Characteristics). Figure D shows that in three-quarters of PCTs less than four in 10 eligible patients are receiving treatment and that in one-third of these PCTs less than two in every 10 eligible patients are receiving therapy.

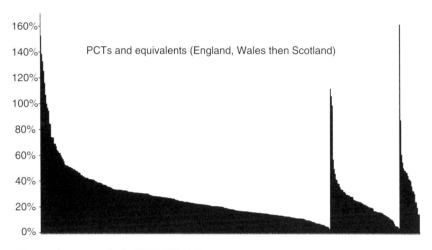

Obese patient penetration by PCO/LHCC/LHB

Figure D   Obesity drugs: patient penetration.

NICE guidance for pegylated interferons was issued in January 2004 for pegylated interferon alfa-2a (Pegasys) and pegylated interferon alfa-2b (ViraferonPeg®). Since the guidance was issued almost one year ago there has been little change in the prescribing of these drugs compared against the overall eligible patient pool described within the NICE guidance (*see* Figure E). One reason for this is because at present there are many undiagnosed hepatitis C patients within the UK, and generally only limited treatment facilities and services are available in relatively small numbers of specialist centres.

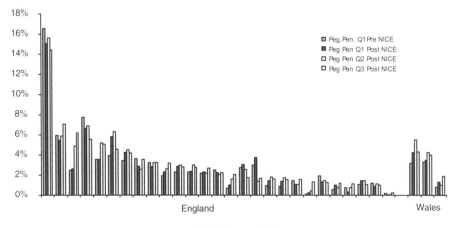

StHAs/former ROs

Figure E   Pegylated interferons: patient penetration.

Conclusion

The implementation of NICE guidance is changing the dynamics of prescribing within England and Wales. For most of the drugs included within the Roche audits, particularly the cancer drugs which each bring a demonstrated survival advantage, it is clear that many more eligible patients are now being given access to treatments which have been established by NICE as being both clinically and cost-effective. In many areas, those NHS organisations implementing NICE guidance most effectively are achieving levels of uptake which are comparable to many other European countries. However, there remains considerable inequity and variation across the country in terms of the use of these products. The challenge which now lies ahead involves providing appropriate support, and sharing best practice, so that all NHS organisations charged with implementing NICE guidance can do so in a timely and effective manner.

PART SEVEN

Achieving quality in public health

Preventing falls in older people

Maurice Wilson

As a volunteer with the Healthy Communities Collaborative in Northampton, I have been actively engaged in planning and executing changes within my local community in relation to two major projects instigated and managed by the Primary Care Trust Development Team – 'prevention of falls in older people' and 'nutrition'.

Preventing falls

Our local slogan was ' Watch your step', for which we arranged 'Happy Feet' days at local GP surgeries, exercise classes in community centres, and a roadshow which was taken to local groups and residential homes. These events aimed to put over some of the main messages about falls such as inactivity, poor lighting, hazardous footwear, untidy floors, etc. through an entertainment of song and dance.

The success of this project rested largely upon the method of 'plan, do, study, act' (PDSA). This placed the onus for action upon community volunteers who could plan change mechanisms relevant to our own areas and community groups, and yet enable us to work in equal partnership with health professionals. The beauty of the project was that it was 'action-based', which meant success rested with community volunteers themselves: it was about people feeling included in any change and their contributions and opinions being valued.

Falls prevention was a fairly straightforward project and its impact easy to measure: we were successful in reducing the incidence of falls by 31% over a 12-month period.

Nutrition

The second project, in which we are currently engaged, is 'nutrition'. I felt from the start that this would be much more difficult both to instigate and measure. There are already many organisations working in this area and many do not seem to communicate with each other. Besides this, messages about food are often conflicting and ever-changing. To alter people's eating habits is a long-term project and it seemed unlikely that we would make a noticeable difference in a year.

We were given a kick-start by the Primary Care Trust Development Team, who directed us to our first 'PDSA'. This involved mapping the availability of food retail outlets in our area. We then added to this by mapping associated factors such as breakfast clubs, lunch clubs, allotments, mobile shops, etc. This was hard work and involved much foot slogging; but it was useful in that it gave us knowledge about the local situation and a good basis on which to build. We followed this by asking local people whether they had problems in accessing fresh food and found that over 30% indicated inaccessibility of fresh fish. We targeted this in our next PDSA and arranged for a mobile fish supplier to extend his round to our area.

At this point I took a course at our local catering college designed to train people to cook on a budget. It was not a good course but I learned much through observation; particularly the need to work with individuals, the need to utilise the skills of students, how to deal with failures, etc. I decided to make use of this knowledge in the 'nutrition' project by putting on free courses on cooking healthy meals on the cheap. Initially we decided to target widowers who had been left without the necessary skills when their wives had died.

The media took an interest in this and it came to the attention of John Reid, the Secretary of State for Health, which gave it a high profile. Some of the people I deal with had been turned off by 'the professionals' during their lives, so it was important to keep it low-key and very localised. We targeted small groups in local community venues (church halls, community centres and the like) to which they would have easy access and where they could feel comfortable with facilities largely replicating those found in the home (a cooker, a fridge and a kitchen sink).

The aim of each session was to develop their cooking skills, to help them gain confidence, to improve the quality of their food, to encourage experimentation and to learn budgeting and shopping skills. Factors such as nutrition and food hygiene were dealt with incidentally. Dishes were simple – cheap and nutritious – with a main course costing around 75p and a dessert or soup costing around 25p. They took home a meal in a foil container either to reheat or freeze.

I have found that inhibitors to a healthy diet for people in this age range arise from a diversity of factors other than lack of skill – social, psychological and environmental factors play an important part. Consequently I try to make it fun, and pair them off to help break social isolation and hopefully nurture a more lasting social bond.

We have had a range of requests to extend this facility to other groups – young offenders, students, young mothers, the unemployed, mental health groups and so on. What I do can be adapted to any client group, so our next task, and the most urgent, is to set up our own courses to train a group of local volunteers who can be called upon to run sessions and help spread and extend the work. The local social services department is already considering offering this as an alternative to 'meals on wheels' for some clients. There are so many development possibilities from this initial action which sprung originally from the community itself.

Public health, primary care and quality

Andrew Scott-Clark

The workshop aimed to ensure an understanding of public health practice in the UK and to explore the current opportunities around public health, primary care and quality. We discussed and considered some of the key national initiatives and policy drivers of primary care in this context. The workshop also picked up the key themes of the recently published Public Health White Paper, particularly around primary prevention and individuals.

Introduction

Public health is defined by the Faculty of Public Health as:

- The science and art of preventing disease, prolonged life and promoting, protecting and improving health through the organised efforts of society.

The Public health approach is population-based, emphasises the collective responsibility for health, its protection and disease prevention, recognises the key role of the state, has a multidisciplinary basis incorporating both quantitative and qualitative methods and emphasises partnerships with all those who contribute to the health of the population.

The three key domains of public health include Health Protection, Health Improvement and Health & Social Care, all of which are underpinned by the surveillance and monitoring of health and determinants of health.

Determinants of health

The Dahlgren and Whitehead model of health determinants describes health being influenced on a numbers of layers including lifestyle, social and community networks, living and working conditions, and finally by general socio-economic and cultural factors. We also need to think about the structure of populations (whatever population we consider) and consider the individuals that make up that population.

White Paper

The recent Public Health White Paper *Choosing Health: Making Healthier Choices* picks up the theme of the individual. The underpinning principles include informed choice, personalisation and working together. The overriding aim is to make the NHS a 'health service' rather than an 'illness' service.

Primary care

When considering primary care, we concentrated on the NHS independent contracted services: GMS, GDS, General Ophthalmic Services and Pharmaceutical Services. Primary care is clearly much broader than these services, but this is a good starting place.

General Medical Services

The new GP contract, recently introduced, moves away from payments being made on the basis of number of patients being registered to one that is based more upon improving quality of care. The central pillar of the new contract is the QOF, a framework that rewards practices for good practice through participation in an annual quality improvement cycle.

- The framework represents the first time any large health system in any country will systematically reward practices on the basis of the quality of care delivered to patients

BMA, February 2003

The framework is divided into four domains:

1 clinical (CHD, stroke and TIA, hypertension, hypothyroidism, diabetes, mental health, COPD, asthma, epilepsy, cancer)
2 organisational
3 additional services
4 patient experience.

The focus upon quality of care will undoubtedly benefit the whole practice population. General practice will be working systematically to review the whole practice population rather than just those people who see their GP.

PCTs will also be able to commission further services through Directed Enhanced services, National Enhanced services and Local Enhanced services.

Some of the public health benefits of the new contract are:

- accurate prevalence rates allowing for surveillance, monitoring and planning
- information on chronic disease management
- improved quality of care for individuals
- opportunities for systematic primary and secondary prevention and tertiary prevention.

General Pharmaceutical Services

The traditional community pharmacy contract emphasised the volume of and throughput of prescriptions and hasn't supported the pharmacist's role in reducing dispensing of unnecessary prescriptions. This has led some people to voice concerns over an under utilised resource.

The DH has recently renegotiated a new contract, which focuses on the services pharmacists can provide, with payments increasingly being directed towards quality.

The framework provides legalisation into essential, advanced and enhanced services. Essential services include: dispensing, repeat dispensing, disposal of medicines, promotion of healthy lifestyles, promotion of self-care for patients with minor ailments and signposting for patients to other healthcare provision. Clinical governance and CPD will underpin these services.

Advanced services are those that require accreditation of the pharmacists providing the service and/or specific requirements to be met in regard to premises.

Enhanced services are local services that will be commissioned by PCTs according to local needs. This will provide opportunities to contract to provide systematic services which address health inequalities and lifestyles.

Additionally, the DH is sponsoring the development of a Pharmaceutical Public Health Strategy, which is due to be published early in 2005.

General Dental Services

Oral health continues to improve across the UK, but much like other health inequalities, poor oral health is associated with deprivation.

The main concern of the NHS in recent years is to provide core dental services. A recent report by the Chief Dental Officer (*NHS Dentistry: Delivery Changes*, July 2004) mostly addressed issues of working arrangements, recruitment and contractual arrangements. New working arrangements are to be implemented from October 2005 and it is envisaged that this will enable refocus on disease prevention.

General Optical Services

The first report of the National Eye Care Services Steering Group, set up to develop proposals for the modernisation of NHS eye care services, maintaining and developing an integrated, patient-centred service and improving access, choice, working times and quality for all sectors of the community.

Priority has been to develop model care pathways for:

- cataract
- glaucoma
- low vision
- age-related macular degeneration (ARMD).

It is unclear how future optical services will develop, but there is no doubt that systematic care and quality will remain the focus.

Conclusion

The primary care landscape is changing rapidly, with public health taking centre stage. Quality is also at the centre, with new primary care contracts focusing on systematic health improvement, reduction in health inequalities, health protection and harm minimisation.

Developing the 'smokefree hospital'

Bryan Stoten

Background

The University Hospitals Coventry and Warwickshire NHS Trust provides acute hospital care across three sites in Coventry city centre, Rugby and on the Coventry and Warwickshire border. It is in the throes of building a £360 million new hospital that will provide tertiary and secondary care for a population in excess of one million people serving a mixed population of affluent (and very non-affluent) rural dwellers together with a largely industrial working-class urban community. Smoking rates across the local health economy are slightly in excess of the national average with 35% of over-35-year-old male mortality attributable to tobacco-related diseases.

In mid-2003 the HDA approached the Trust offering financial support for a 'smokefree hospital' initiative. The Trust's Senior Management Team including its Chairman were all committed to the Tobacco Control Agenda.

In agreement with the HDA and the Government Office the Trust set its objectives: to secure smokefree hospital buildings with no-smoking facilities together with the provision of smoking shelters provided 50 metres from the buildings for staff on official breaks and members of the public. A Smoking and Health Group was established meeting monthly. The membership of the group was multidisciplinary. The HDA maintained regular contact with the group. Three subgroups were set up: A **staff issues** group supported by those active in providing a smoking cessation service; a **patient issues** group drawing from nursing and smoking cessation advisers together with the Director of Pharmacy and the Medical Director responsible for training staff on how to inform patients of the policy changes; and an **estates** group tasked with auditing all hospital sites to identify existing smoking rooms which would be closed and the appropriate sites for smoking shelters in the grounds of the hospitals.

Early on in the programme staff were informed of the new policy through a leaflet issued together with payslips, which also offered smoking cessation classes and nicotine replacement therapy provision. The actual launch in April 2004 resulted in the closure of many smoking rooms but was interrupted by a change in the policy introduced as a result of a direction from the SHA. This was coupled with the advice from the CMO that smokefree sites rather than merely smokefree hospitals were desirable and this change resulted in a decision not to provide smoking shelters on the hospital sites. It was argued at the time that the expenditure (in the region of £60 000) was indefensible for behaviours that were known to be damaging both to the smokers themselves and those with whom they came into contact.

The actualité

By the summer of 2004 a meeting held between the Chairman of the Trust and the trade union representatives resulted in agreement to write individually to all staff members giving the rationale for the hospital sites becoming smokefree as justified in health and safety terms, focusing particularly on the dangers inherent in second-hand smoke and the importance of health service professionals not being seen to engage in behaviours harmful to health.

It is clear that the delay both in communicating with staff and in removing the remaining smoking shelters was due to anxiety about the impact of such action on other Trust priorities. The pressures to meet elective surgery waiting-time targets, the pressure on accident and emergency staff to satisfactorily meet the four-hour waiting target and the collaboration required of the unions in preparing for the introduction of *Agenda for Change* made human resource managers sensitive to any further pressures which they felt staff might take negatively.

Whilst these sensitive issues were being 'juggled' rather than negotiated the external environment changed dramatically.

The Smokefree Workplace Initiative introduced by the Irish government earlier in the year added to the pressure that the Government was coming under to introduce similar policies through the publication of its Public Health White Paper expected from June 2004 onwards. The views of the Chief Medical Officer were widely known throughout the NHS and in the case of the University Hospital Trust were given further support by both verbal and then, later, written instructions from the SHA.

The first phase of implementation – removing most but not all of the patient's smoking rooms and the staff smoking shelters, together with the provision of smoking cessation programmes, had gone without protest. However, in this success lay other difficulties provoked by non-smoking staff. As the normative culture changed, so non-smoking staff became more vociferous. A series of 'back to the floor' meetings between frontline staff and the senior managers of the Trust resulted in further calls for a smokefree environment. Senior management had understood the closure of smoking rooms to have gone further than was in fact the case. Furthermore, the apparently inexplicable delay in removing external smoking shelters, which had become provocative in the new climate, so supportive of smokefree workplaces, resulted in increasing management frustration. Eventually, after a series of inconclusive discussions with the trade unions and a further individual communication to every member of staff, the decision was unilaterally taken to close the five remaining smoking rooms across the Trust's sites together with the demolition of external staff shelter. This was accomplished within 24 hours of the instruction being given.

The 'backlash'

The final step which resulted in the removal of all smoking facilities on the hospital sites, coupled with the erection of smokefree signage, both internally and externally, resulted in little protest. Twelve members of staff engaged in a short 'smoke-out' outside the administration block of the Trust. A petition gathered 200 names and the Trust Chairman and Chief Executive received two congratulatory emails!

The paradox

Having gone so far so fast, what lessons can we draw from the experience?

- Preparation to introduce tobacco control measures was crucially important in securing goodwill and trust from staff who were smokers but wished to quit and from those who intended to continue as smokers.
- The Trust made clear from the beginning that it was not intending to be punitive but was asking staff who smoked to behave as responsible health-care professionals, restricting their smoking behaviour to non-working time.
- Staff were presented both with the health and safety issues and the issues that as a healthcare institution staff had a higher responsibility to their patients than they might have in other employment.
- Constant engagement with the unions even though not resulting in agreement made the final unilateral decision palatable to staff representatives and resulted in little ultimate protest.
- In particular we learnt two lessons – first, that preparation, communication, training, support and environmental changes including reduced facilities for smoking and enhanced signage all create a climate in which the final sanction becomes acceptable. Second, it was clear that a total end to accepting smoking on the site could only be achieved by decisive action. A 'mopping up' exercise appeared to be one which could stretch on for a long time. The ultimate exercise of management prerogative brought about a formal end to a behaviour which, denied any legitimacy within the organisation, is now of insignificant importance.

The change in the cultural assumptions of the organisation have been achieved in a period of little more than 12 months – certainly helped by the changed national climate and the public debate around smokefree workplaces, but delivered through a mixture of explanation and consultation together with, ultimately, decisive management action.

PART EIGHT

Patient safety and clinical risk

Implementing guidance of safe medication practice

David Cousins

The problem

Case reports in UK[1–12] and worldwide identified deaths and serious patient harm following unintended intravenous administration of potassium chloride concentrate injections. These incidents were caused by potassium chloride concentrate ampoules being mis-selected for sodium chloride and water for injections ampoules, being incompletely mixed when diluted and being temporarily stored and administered in unlabelled syringes.

Developing guidance

Visits to NHS hospitals were conducted to determine the risk factors and safety controls already in place. Information was collected from the UK and elsewhere to identify risk management methods that had been used successfully to control these risks.[13,14] There was little clinical need requiring the storage and use of potassium chloride concentrate on general wards. The maximum concentration of potassium chloride that can be administered via peripheral venous line is 40 mmol/litre. Potassium chloride concentrate ampoules had to be diluted into 500 ml and 1000 ml infusion bags before use and commercially available infusions at ready-to-administer concentrations were available. There are clinical requirements for stronger infusions of potassium chloride via central venous lines in critical care areas. Some NHS hospitals had already introduced supply and storage restrictions on potassium chloride concentrate ampoules to ensure they were not stored alongside diluent ampoules.

Guidance on safe medication practice

The NPSA issued a Patient Safety Alert to the NHS in July 2002 requiring prompt action to address this high-risk safety problem. The alert was for the attention of Chief Executives of NHS Trusts and PCTs and for action by Chief Pharmacists and Pharmaceutical Advisers in NHS Trusts and PCTs.

Eight actions were required:

1 Restriction on the clinical areas holding stocks of potassium chloride concentrate.
2 Requirement for potassium chloride concentrate to be stored in a separate locked cupboard.
3 Restriction of transfer of potassium chloride concentrate between clinical areas.
4 Documentation control on potassium chloride concentrate.
5 Approved range of potassium chloride infusion – promoting ready-to-use where possible.
6 Requirement for the preparation of infusions with potassium chloride concentrate to have a second check from another practitioner.
7 Staff training associated with risks of potassium chloride concentrate.
8 Procedure for the supply of potassium chloride out-of-hours

Evaluation

The NPSA conducted two Sharing and Learning Exercises in December 2002 and December 2003 to determine progress with implementation. Hospital Chief Pharmacists were invited to complete a questionnaire to determine implementation of recommendations, changes in product usage and storage, and the costs of implementing the changes.

In 2002, 166 out of 195 (85%) Hospital Trusts in England and Wales responded to the questionnaire. In 2003, 150 out of 181 (83%) responded to the questionnaire.

The questionnaire indicated that before the alert only 25% of Trusts had all the NPSA-recommended risk management controls in place. This had increased to 69% six months after the alert and 87% 18 months after the alert.

More detailed results indicated that 98% of the Trusts had restricted the clinical areas that could hold potassium chloride concentrate as ward stock. In the majority of wards the concentrate had been removed and ready-to-administer infusions of potassium chloride were now used, and these infusions minimised the risks for patients.

In 97% of Trusts the critical care areas that still required to use potassium chloride concentrate stored the potassium chloride ampoules in separate locked cupboards from plain diluent ampoules to minimise mis-selection errors.

Product usage information indicated that the use of potassium chloride concentrate had reduced by 16–27% in the reporting Trusts over 18 months. At the same time, the usage of potassium chloride infusions (up to 40 mmol/litre) had increased by 17–45%. The use of more concentrated infusions (greater than 40 mmol/litre) available as unlicensed specials, intended to replace the use of the concentrate ampoules in critical care areas, increased by 212–222%.

The NPSA is working with the NHS Purchasing and Supplies Agency, the Medicines and Healthcare Products Regulatory Agency and the pharmaceutical industry to obtain supplies of some of these 'specials' as fully licensed medicine products in the future.

The implementation of NPSA guidance has reduced the risks of patient safety incidents involving potassium chloride in NHS hospitals in England and Wales.

Reference

1   Cousins DH and Upton DR (2000) Medication Errors: Is it time to make strong KCl a controlled drug? *Pharmacy in Practice* **10**: 187.

2   Cousins DH and Upton DR (1999) Medication Errors: Proceed with caution in Critical Care. *Pharmacy in Practice* **9**: 132.

3   Cousins DH and Upton DR (1996) Medication Errors : Act now to prevent KCL deaths. *Pharmacy in Practice* **6**: 307–10.

4   Cousins DH and Upton DR (1995) Medication Errors: Lethal drug ampoules still being issued to wards? *Pharmacy in Practice* **5**: 130.

5   Anon (1994) Case history 3. Injection error. *Journal of the Medical Defence Union* **10**: 19.

6   Cousins DH and Upton DR (1994) Medication Errors: Stop these parenteral blunders. *Hospital Pharmacy Practice* **4**: 388–90.

7   Shanker KB, Palkar NV and Nishala R (1985) Paraplegia following epidural potassium chloride. *Anaesthesia* **40**: 45–7.

8   Lakhani M, Stewart WK (1985) Hazards of potassium chloride solutions. *The Lancet* **2**: 453.

9   Rendell-Baker L and Meyer JA (1985) Hazards of potassium chloride solutions. *The Lancet* **2**: 329.

10 Mander GA (1985) Hazards of potassium chloride solutions. *The Lancet* **2**: 453.

11 Hawkins C (1985) Hazards of potassium chloride solutions. *The Lancet* **2**: 552.

12 Williams RHP (1973) Potassium overdosage: a potential hazard of non acid parenteral fluid containers. *BMJ* **1**: 714–15.

13 Anon (2001) Patient Safety Alert: Medication error prevention: potassium chloride. *International Journal of Quality in Health Care* **23**: 155.

14 Swanson D (2003) Implementing an IV potassium policy. *Pharm J.* **10**: 348–52.

The miracle of the general practice consultation

Roger Neighbour

What miracle?

Every day over a million patients see a GP. Over 80% of consultations will be rated by patients as substantially meeting their needs, and – the occasional high-profile case notwithstanding – very, very few will go wrong. In less than 10 minutes, not only will acute or chronic clinical agendas be dealt with, but psychological, social, preventative, administrative, educational and pastoral issues tackled as well. Moreover, all this will be achieved at a lower financial cost than in most other developed countries.

The miracle is that so few can do so much for so many so safely, so efficiently and so cheaply.

How is the miracle achieved?

First, by understanding some key differences between the ways specialists and generalists 'do medicine'. Second, by understanding and making use of the properties of the doctor–patient relationship.

Differences between the specialist and the generalist approach

All patients' medical problems are a mix of the biological, the psychological and the social. They are compounded by patients' differing personalities, health understanding, expectations and beliefs. Their causes are frequently complex and their management seldom clear-cut. Doctors, as well as being skilled professionals, are also human beings with varying skills, emotions and motivations.

At medical school we learn the 'specialist' way of doing medicine, which aims – by thinking convergently, and being systematic and thorough – to diagnose and manage the clinical problem with as much certainty as possible. Specialists usually try to keep to a minimum the potentially distracting effects of the patient's (and the doctor's) individual personalities. The challenge for specialists is to avoid error in defining the problem despite the idiosyncratic ways patients and diseases can behave.

In general practice, however, things have to be done differently, not least because there isn't as much time, or as easy access to investigation, as in the specialist setting. Problems in general practice tend to be less well defined and more multifaceted, calling for more divergent thought processes. Patients expect to be acknowledged as individuals first, and as the victims of pathology second. GPs have to work with lower grade information: histories that are often vague or inconsistent; diseases presenting at very early stages of evolution; complex processes of cause and effect that don't always fit neatly into a biomedical framework. They may have to settle for the least risky, rather than the most rational, course of management. Not least, the consulting room is a place where, over time, doctor and patient build a trusting and confiding personal relationship. The doctor cannot avoid his or her own human reactions becoming a factor in every consultation.

It is important not to overemphasise these differences, which are summarised in Table A. Medicine is an art as well as a science for both specialists and generalists. Clinical competence is essential for both. Both try to bring science and resources to the needs of individual patients. But – and this is the key difference – in the general practice consultation, the doctor is a participant and not just an observer.

Table A The specialist and the generalist ways

The 'specialist' way is to:	The 'generalist' way is to:
• *reduce* uncertainty	• *tolerate* uncertainty
• eradicate observer error	• *work with* observer error
• think *convergently*	• think *divergently*
• *analyse* complexity	• *celebrate* complexity
• achieve '*focused*' problems	• tolerate '*fuzzy*' problems
• minimise diagnostic *error*	• minimise management *risk*
• be *challenged* by individual variation and atypicality	• be *legitimated* by individual variation and atypicality

The dissecting room 'click'

As students we are often told, 'Don't get involved in patients' problems. Stay detached.' And sometimes, because many of the things we see and do are hard to bear, this is necessary advice. Michael Crichton, author of *Jurassic Park*, recalling when as a medical student he had to bisect a cadaver's head with a fretsaw, described how, 'Somewhere inside me there was a kind of click, a shutting off, a refusal to acknowledge what I was doing. After that click I was all right. This shutting-off click was essential to becoming a doctor. You could not function if you were overwhelmed by what was happening.'[1]

But the miracle of an effective consultation is to discover that whatever Crichton's 'click' was switching off – the doctor's own reactions and feelings – it can be safe to switch back on again. Staying uninvolved in what is happening is not the only option.

The miraculous potential of the doctor–patient relationship

Very complicated systems can develop 'emergent properties', which could not have been predicted from studying their components. The 'information revolution' of the Internet is an emergent property of linked computers. Consciousness is an emergent property of a brain-sized conglomeration of neurones.

The doctor–patient relationship has emergent properties. Take the limitless range of clinical problems that patients present; broaden the remit of the consultation to include patients' worries, hopes and sadnesses, issues of housing, poverty, inequalities and injustice; and finally allow the doctor's own personal qualities and responses to be part of the mix and something miraculous happens. The relationship itself becomes an instrument of diagnosis and treatment. The consulting room becomes a crucible. The process that unfolds like a subtext to the clinical dialogue itself adds a dimension of understanding. How each party reacts to the other in a choreography of transference and countertransference suggests, in microcosm, the significance of circumstances and events in the patient's life beyond the surgery, which in turn illuminates how the patient deals with illness, real or perceived.

The doctor, too, can acquire symbolic roles of great therapeutic power: parent, confessor, friend, enemy, lover. The *person* of the doctor has many of the properties of a drug: indications and contraindications; effects, side-effects and interactions; dosage, therapeutic range and overdose risk; dependency and addiction potential; placebo effect. Even in merely practical terms, the trust that grows from a relationship where these factors are recognised contributes to the cost-effectiveness of the British system of primary care, by enhancing compliance, increasing patient satisfaction, reducing unnecessary investigations and referrals, and maintaining doctors' job satisfaction.

Combining these 'generalist' dimensions with 'specialist' biomedical skills endows the consultation with the depth, range and flexibility needed to bring about the '10-minute miracle'.

Reference

1   Crichton M (2002) *Travels*. HarperCollins (Perennial imprint): San Francisco, p. 11.

Local implementation of new interventional procedures

Barrie D White

Background

Before July 2001 'Surgeons were able to introduce new techniques without any formal system of notification and without need to demonstrate the necessary level of skill' and 'There was no requirement for hospital clinicians to keep their skills and knowledge up to date, nor to demonstrate to anyone other than their peer group that they remain sufficiently skilled'. The Kennedy report,[1] from which the quotes are taken, called for local research and ethics committees to address these deficiencies, and reinforced the need for patient information about every aspect of treatment including the individual clinician's experience.[1] The Department of Health (DH) placed these responsibilities with the National Institute for Clinical Excellence (NICE), superseding the voluntary Safety and Efficacy Register of New Interventional Procedures (SERNIP), run by the Academy of Medical Colleges since 1996.[2]

NICE was asked to issue guidance about new procedures. Trusts were expected to design their own methods for the safe introduction of new procedures, such as those 'that a clinician has read about, heard about, or piloted and is not logged in the NHS read codes' or 'one that has not previously been used in that particular hospital or health service'. External inspectorates (CHI/CHAI/Healthcare Commission, CNST) would ensure success.

Method

The experience at University Hospital, Queen's Medical Centre, Nottingham was as follows:

1 The introduction of a Trust policy was simple. A request form to introduce new procedures was produced. The requirement for clinicians to notify new procedures was quickly disseminated. The Trust box could be ticked, leaving the responsibility with clinicians, but this fell far short of assuring competence in every case.

2 Despite many medical conferences describing innovative procedures, clinicians believed few required registration, claiming that they were no longer new, that they were minor modifications or adjuncts to existing procedures, or otherwise outside the remit of the policy.

3 Tack was changed and each clinician was asked to consider the original SERNIP list of 242 procedures inherited by NICE and simply state which of these they did, or confirm that they did none. A register was compiled and repeated reminders gradually permitted a profile of SERNIP procedures to be constructed. The Trust was thus assured that every clinician had at least received the policy and was aware of their responsibilities.

4 As the NICE Interventional Procedure Guidance (IPG) began to be issued in July 2003, clinicians already signed up to SERNIP equivalents were asked to complete the Trust form. This requires evidence of training and competence, examples of the information given to patients (including NICE leaflets), an assurance that the status of the procedure will be discussed and individual results disclosed, a specimen consent form, an agreement that untoward incidents will be reported by the normal Trust mechanisms and (for procedures with audit requirements) an obligation to submit data to national registries where they exist, or the CHI-commended QMC Enquiry into Patient Outcomes and Deaths (QEPOD) where they do not.

5 Procedures which NICE judges to be part of routine practice and permissible within the normal arrangements for consent and audit, are considered by the clinician's directorate governance group (including the Clinical Director) and signed off by the Divisional Assistant Medical Director (who has corporate responsibility for clinical governance). These submissions are ratified by the Medical Director and sent as an item for information to the Trust's Clinical Governance Committee. For procedures with cautionary guidance the Medical Director additionally interviews the clinician, and the Trust's Clinical Governance Committee ratifies the request. New procedures without NICE guidance are treated as cautionary guidance requests.

6 Clinicians meeting the necessary requirements are issued with certificates on which are described and accepted their commitments to explain the procedure, supply information, obtain consent, report incidents and audit outcomes appropriately.

7 A master matrix of every procedure (new, new to the Trust, new to the clinician, SERNIP, NICE, etc.) and every clinician's response (no response, no procedures, procedures requested, credentialed for, etc.) is available on the hospital's intranet with hyperlinks to individual NICE guidance subdivided by type into proscribed, research only, cautionary, normal practice with conditions and normal practice (Table A).

8 NICE procedures, in their public consultation period, are notified to all clinicians who are invited to contribute and register their interest. NICE guidance is sent to every clinician as it is published, with reminders to register where appropriate.

9 Clinicians are encouraged to publicise their innovative contributions. All

Table A

Clinician	Division	Specialty	Procedure	Identifier	NICE Status	New	New to trust	New to clinician	NICE notified	Trust notified	Trust status	Clinician status
—	Surgery	Ophth	Scleral expansion surgery for presbyopia	IPG070	Not to be used							
—	Medicine	Gastro	Photodynamic therapy for high-grade dysplasia in Barrett's oesophagus	IPG082	Normal practice							
MNB	Surgery	Maxfac	Customised titanium implants for orofacial reconstruction	IPG028	Research only	NO	NO	NO	NO	NO		
KJH	D & F	Radiology	Stent-graft placement in abdominal aortic aneurysm	IPG010	Special arrangements	NO	NO	NO	NO	YES		Trainer
JHG	Surgery	Vascular	Stent-graft placement in abdominal aortic aneurysm	IPG010	Special arrangements	NO	NO	NO	NO	YES		Trained
KJH	D & F	Radiology	Uterine artery embolisation for the treatment of fibroids	IPG094 See also IPG001	Normal practice outcomes to www.bsir.org	NO	NO	NO	NO	YES		Trained
FDS	D & F	Radiology	Percutaneous vertebroplasty	IPG012	Normal practice	NO	NO	NO	NO	YES		Trained
APO	Surgery	Vascular	Stent-graft placement in thoracic aorta	SERNIP		NO	YES	YES	NO	YES		Transfer
HGF	Surgery	T & O	Viscosupplementation for osteoarthritis of knee (Synvisc)	SERNIP		NO	YES	YES	NO	YES		Training
TRE	Medicine	Gen Med	Bronchial needle aspiration	Trust		NO	Yes	NO	NO	YES		Training
WIE	Surgery	Neurosurg	Artificial cervical disc replacement	Trust		NO	NO	YES	YES	YES		Training
WIE	Surgery	Neurosurg	Partial cervical discectomy	New		YES	NO	NO	YES	YES		Training
REW	Surgery	Neurosurg	None	T								
NBV	D & F	Pathology	No Response	T								

members of staff are expected to ensure that clinicians are certificated for new/NICE procedures, and are challenged where this seems not to be the case. Theatres, sterile services, radiology and endoscopy suites have been targeted to ensure that new/NICE procedures are brought to the attention of the Trust. Clinical coders are similarly asked to identify NICE procedures (using IPG codes in the QEPOD form) to complete the audit trail.

Regulatory change

Local implementation of these mechanisms has not been easy. NICE began this work in April 2002. Since then its website has matured, and the definition of 'new procedure' has been refined. Guidance to surgeons was published in September 2002,[3] and to Trusts in November 2003.[4] In June 2004 NICE announced a programme to support implementation of its guidance, but unfortunately the DH made no mention of interventional procedures in its accompanying directive.[5] Standards for Better Health place the (conspicuously absent in first draft) interventional programme at the core of patient safety,[6] and CNST now requires evidence of a clear policy and training records for new procedures.[7] The fact that at least one medical defence organisation requests notification of NICE procedures[8] (with the implication that non-declaration might mean no indemnity) has probably done more than the rest to engage clinicians.

Conclusion

To prevent harm coming to patients from inappropriate treatments or inadequately trained clinicians is a laudable ambition, but a difficult task. The lack of central guidance, the rapid pace of change and the uncertain direction of development do not make it easier. Measuring competence is a major challenge at any point in a career. We have made a start with NICE and now its new interventional procedures programme. Established practice must follow.

References

1   Secretary of State for Health (2001) *Learning from Bristol. The Report of the Public Inquiry into children's heart surgery at the Bristol Royal Infirmary 1984–1995*. The Stationery Office: London.

2   Department of Health (2002) *Learning from Bristol: The Department of Health's Response to the Report of the Public Inquiry into children's heart surgery at the Bristol Royal Infirmary 1984–1995*. DOH: London.

3   The Royal College of Surgeons of England (2002) *Good Surgical Practice*. The Royal College of Surgeons of England: London.

4   Department of Health (2003) *The Interventional Procedures Programme*. Health Service Circular HSC2003/011. DOH: London.

5   Lord Warner and the Department of Health (2004) *Implementation of NICE Guidance*. DOH: London.

6   Department of Health (2004) *Standards for Better Health*. DOH: London.

7   Clinical Negligence Scheme for Trusts (2004) *Clinical Risk Management Standards*. NHS Litigation Authority.

8   Medical Defence Union (2004) *Risk Management Questionnaire for Consultants (General Surgery)*.

Improving the introduction of new interventional procedures: the Leicester experience

Keith Blanshard

A clear framework has been set by NICE to guide the introduction of new interventional procedures; and each Trust will require a process to ensure compliance with the policy and Health Services Circular 2003/11.

A procedure new to the Trust or clinician may, or may not, carry supporting external guidance. However, two important issues face any Acute Trust in the introduction of a new procedure – resources and safety. University Hospitals of Leicester NHS Trust (UHL) continues to carry out considerable work with the local health community to ensure resource issues for new interventional procedures are addressed. The focus of this presentation is concerned with improving patient safety and encouraging innovation.

There is an inevitable balance between ensuring patient safety and encouraging innovation, and any control of new interventional procedure introduction requires clinical support and understanding to succeed. Within UHL the New Interventional Procedures Advisory Group (NIPAG), constituted in October 2003, supports clinicians and clinical directors (CD). The CD retains executive authority, appropriately, since there may be resource implications. Membership of NIPAG reflects the balance between corporate and clinical responsibility (including innovation where needed). Members include the Director and Assistant Director of Clinical Governance (thus also encompassing the Patient Safety Group), the corporate directorates of Education, Corporate and Legal Affairs. The Research and Development Directorate and Nurses are also represented. In addition there are eight clinicians, representing a cross-section of the Clinical Directorates.

Notifications are invited from interested clinicians, supported by an evidence base for the proposed intervention, and including proposals for training (both the individual and the team), properly informed patient consent, evidence of audit methodology and timeframe for reporting clinical performance to NIPAG. We also seek specific information around intended proctorship, and an identified specialist adviser from whom the Trust can seek further independent specialist advice.

NIPAG reports to the Trust Clinical Governance Committee (CGC), and the Chair also reports on a bimonthly basis to the Director of Clinical Governance.

NIPAG monitors notifications, audit targets and outcomes, which is enabled by close links with the Clinical Audit, Standards and Effectiveness (CASE) team within the Trust.

Experience has shown that a process of continuous communication is required to maintain awareness and understanding of the role of NIPAG. This has included emailed letters to every clinician within the Trust (over 400 consultants), visits to the Clinical Directorate Board Meetings, their Clinical Governance Meetings, and inclusion in the biannual clinical governance reviews.

During the first year of operation there have been 11 notifications. Five were supported, five were returned with requests for further details, and one was forwarded to the Research and Development Directorate because it was clearly a research project. The CGC and NIPAG continue to monitor the notification rate. Unfortunately, no benchmarking data is available from NICE itself at present. However, preliminary benchmarking with other Acute Trusts within the UK has indicated that our notification or referral rate remains comparable to other similar centres.

The importance of reinforcing the use of NIPAG is underlined by serious adverse events. Two have occurred during the introduction of one supported new interventional procedure. Communication channels were effective and support given to patients and practitioners. The procedure was stopped pending a review and report on the serious adverse events. A root cause analysis was also undertaken and a resubmission to NIPAG will be required before restarting the procedure can be supported.

Some of the problems that have been encountered include a definition of a 'new' procedure, and the reqirement to support the process (which is resource-intensive).

Keys to success include maintaining a profile and dialogue with clinicians and responding quickly. The fundamental principles require reiteration to reassure clinicians and to ensure the group retains a balanced approach.

Any such Group is well advised to insist on sight of properly prepared information leaflets to underpin a high standard of well-informed patient consent. The signature of an independent supporting CD is essential, and evidence of NICE notification essential to inform the Group. Training the team underpins the success of any new interventional procedure, and defining and structuring the training for a specific new procedure continues to remain an important challenge.

Involving clinicians in risk management

John HB Scarpello

Reports from the United States, Australia and Europe are consistent and show that adverse clinical events involve around 10% of hospital admissions. Not all of these adverse events are severe, and the projected national figures have to be interpreted with caution since they have been extrapolated from modest samples. Nevertheless, conservative estimates from the United States suggest that between 44 000 and 98 000 deaths occur each year as a result of medical errors; and in the United Kingdom hospital-acquired infections are estimated to cost £1 billion per annum. The high frequency of errors in clinical practice should not be a surprise. Healthcare is self-evidently a complex process. Every illness is unique to an individual and most clinical conditions provide challenges in diagnosis, investigation and management. The dynamics of communication and interpersonal skills required by healthcare teams can themselves prove to be a major source of system failure.

In recent years there has been a realisation that in order to improve patient safety, and ensure robust risk management, new paradigms are required. In the past, investigation of clinical error has usually been reactive, often with apportioning of blame to an individual or a clinical team. It is now accepted that in most instances it is weak systems, rather than poor performance, that create the conditions for error. Clinical risk management is complex and requires an understanding of ways for assessing different levels of risk. In order to more fully understand and improve patient safety we need better systems to capture information of both clinical process and outcomes. Subsequent analysis provides the opportunity to learn from error and, wherever possible, to re-design the process to change the system and 'build out' error.

Improving safety is not unique to healthcare. Most industries invest considerable resources into understanding their main areas of risk with the aim of developing fail-safe processes. The airways industry is often cited as a successful example in which serious safety incidents have been reduced as a direct result of a change in culture which now promotes an open and blame-free reporting system. Such industries can provide examples of novel approaches to reducing risk by healthcare providers, especially in relation to improved communication and empowerment by clinical teams. Such human factor engineering is important, but there are many differences between clinical practice and flying an aircraft. Air crew know their destination in advance, and fail-safe mechanisms have been developed over many years. People with acute illness may present to an emergency department confused, in pain or even unconscious. The healthcare team is often working under severe time pressures with little opportunity to reduce or regulate the numbers of patients requiring their attention. In addition, the NHS has introduced artificial targets which are rarely clinically driven and can reduce quality.

Medical science has developed at a dramatic rate over the last half century and the complexity of modern healthcare brings enhanced risks. Risk assessment together with better reporting, analysis and review of safety incidents provides a real opportunity to improve the quality of patient care. The benefits would not only be to the patient and his/her family but also to those providing healthcare, by reducing anxiety and enhancing professional satisfaction. There is also the prospect of major cost savings, both directly (for example, reduced bed-days), and from litigation.

Despite the general acceptance of the importance of safety reporting, the majority of research funding continues to be directed towards understanding pathophysiological mechanisms of disease and to developing novel therapies. In recent years the understanding of the need to establish best evidence in the practice of healthcare has promoted a fundamental change in medical education. Similarly, we need to convince clinicians and clinical managers of the benefits in collecting data of patient safety incidents (including, especially, 'near misses') with the objective of designing solutions to reduce risk.

Patient safety incidents can have a wider impact than on patient care alone. While they can be devastating for the patient they can also profoundly affect the clinicians involved who may lose self-esteem and even be threatened by legal or disciplinary action. As a first step to researching the cause of patient safety incidents, and to developing solutions, the NPSA was established to develop processes for recording information using a national database; and with the objective of learning from the results and developing solutions in order to reduce risks to patients. At present there is a considerable gap between the numbers of incidents revealed by detailed audit and local risk registers. This is a challenge which has to be overcome.

How can individual clinicians and managers be encouraged to increase reporting of errors? We require a cultural change. Clinical teams should devote time at the end of procedures and clinical sessions (for example, a wardround or theatre list), to discuss those aspects of care where errors or near-misses have been found. This would have benefits in more accurate reporting, and provide a multiprofessional educational opportunity which could in turn be seen as reducing any perceived threat to members of the clinical team. At present there is little direct incentive for reporting errors since feedback is often limited. The opportunities provided by the National Reporting and Learning System, developed by the NPSA, will allow access to a wide database with information about any work in progress around the topic of a reported incident.

The profile of patient safety, and an understanding of the basic principles of analysis of error and risk management, need to be incorporated into both undergraduate and continuing postgraduate education for all the professions involved in healthcare delivery. At their annual review clinical staff should be challenged to show how they have reported errors; and what actions they have taken to minimise subsequent risk. The vision of the NPSA is to create a safer NHS. Safety can no longer be regarded as an add-on. It must be integral to all providers of care. We require clinically based and easier reporting systems. A culture change needs to be promoted whereby both patients and providers have confidence in error reporting which comes to be seen as improving long-term patient safety.

Management of a major incident in hospital: how theory was put into practice

Brijendra Shravat

Introduction

Barnet and Chase Farm Hospitals NHS Trust has two acute hospitals with 24-hour Accident and Emergency (A&E) departments situated five miles apart. Both were receiving hospitals for the Potters Bar rail crash. Establishing and maintaining the capability on both sites requires meticulous planning and ongoing teaching and training. The command and control system, general plan and action cards are the same for both sites.

Role of acute hospital

There are five major roles for receiving hospitals during a major incident:[1]

- to provide a clinical response
- to liaise with the ambulance service, other hospitals and agencies in order to manage the impact of the incident
- to maintain communication with relatives and friends of existing patients and those from the incident, the local community, the media and VIPs
- to provide on-site medical care and advice
- to ensure the hospital continues all its essential functions throughout the incident.

Training and exercises

The acute hospital should have an up-to-date major incident plan that considers all foreseeable causes of a major incident, including chemical and biological incidents, and incidents involving radioactivity. In accordance with DH guidelines[1] we have done live exercises to ensure that staff are fully trained and equipped for their roles in a major incident. This also identifies strengths and weaknesses in the plan. The A&E consultant on each site is responsible for collectively updating the Trust-wide major incident plan, preparing the training material for all the Trust including medical and nursing staff as well as managers.

Management of major incident in the hospital

Just before midday on a Friday, a train derailed and crashed at Potters Bar station. The first response was by police, ambulance and fire services, who declared a major incident. The MIO (Medical Incident Officer) to assist with managing the incident at scene and an MMT (Mobile Medical Team) to help with emergency treatment of casualties were requested from a near-by hospital supporting the incident. This meant that main receiving hospitals' (Barnet and Chase Farm Hospitals) capability was not compromised to respond effectively to the incident.

The alerting message came to both A&E departments on the ambulance service hotline. The A&E Nurse In-charge declared a major incident for each hospital via switchboard. The switchboard contacted the key management, medical, nursing, administrative and support staff according to the prearranged and prioritised call-out cascade. As both sites were asked to respond at the same time the senior managers of the organisation were required to split into two separate groups and had to assume the roles of their 'missing' colleagues by following their action cards.

Each key department designated one person to maintain 'cascade' call-out lists for their own staff, which were updated quarterly. The major incident control team (MICT) took command and control of the incident response within Hospital Control Centre (HCC). As outlined in the plan, all elective operations were cancelled. Senior clinicians went with their teams to wards and made beds available by either discharging patients home or by transferring them to peripheral hospitals. The pressure areas were switchboard, A&E, theatres, ITU and imaging facilities. The staff called in reported to HCC.

As the A&E consultant on duty, I took charge as 'Medical Officer in-charge' and was responsible for implementing the medical aspect of the plan and kept direct communication with the MICT and MIO. The A&E Nurse In-charge and myself (silver leaders) coordinated the medical and nursing staff arriving to A&E to all clinical areas in accordance with the major incident plan. All on-call specialty teams including cardiac arrest and trauma teams were called to A&E to assist A&E staff clear all non-urgent cases from the department.

Four trauma teams with named ATLS-trained team leaders were identified for resuscitation bays. A named doctor and nurse were identified for each bay within Majors, and Minors was manned with one doctor and nurse. A senior doctor and a senior nurse coordinated all activity within the resuscitation room and majors area. Our experience shows this assignment of senior medical and nursing staff in key positions within A&E is paramount. The Trust major incident plan designates a senior doctor (Consultant Urologist) as a Clinical Co-ordinator. This ensures that all patients are investigated and treated in priority order which facilitates effective use of resources such as imaging (*see* Figure A).

The communication between Medical Officer In-charge, Clinical Coordinator and A&E Nurse In-charge, all three silver leaders, is key to the smooth running of patients' management within A&E. Our command and control structure closely mirrors that used by the other emergency services and comprises three levels of command:[1] Gold leader (Executive Directors); Silver leader (coordinator of operational and tactical activity) and Bronze leader (delivery of front-line service within specialty).

All casualties entered the A&E department through a single entrance (the other entrances being locked) and were triaged by the Casualty Assessment Officer (second A&E consultant). Receptionists prepared registration documents. Casualties were triaged into three groups: severely injured (ABC compromised) to Resuscitation room; moderate injury (without life-threatening problems) to Majors; walking wounded to Minors.

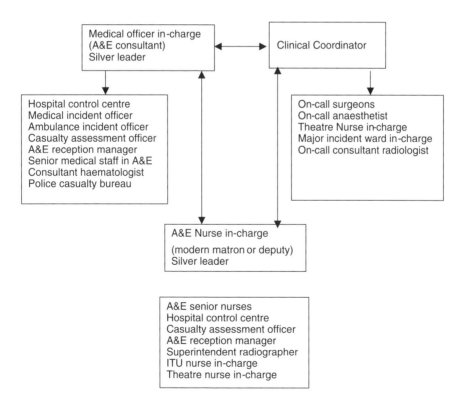

Figure A   Liaison role of three key persons in the A&E department (Silver Team).

Casualties were transferred out of the A&E department to theatre, ITU or the 'major incident designated receiving ward' following appropriate resuscitation and investigations. On this occasion we did not receive any walking wounded but as per plan they would have been transferred to the discharge lounge, where their final condition and documentation would have been checked. This check would identify any necessary follow-up and community support prior to discharge. No patient is discharged home from the A&E department.

Practical difficulties in major incident planning

The major incident plan must be robust and flexible, ensuring our service can cope with any eventuality. There is a thorough debriefing with analysis of events after any major incident, so the lessons learned can be incorporated into the hospital plan. Some difficulties we encountered were:

- Incomplete documentation: The named doctor and nurse were accountable for completing documentation.
- Identity of staff: Not all members of staff wore a tabard or uniform, and it was time-consuming to identify their rank and specialty. A set of different coloured armbands for different specialty staff might help.
- Patient's possessions were occasionally lost during the intense activity of the major incident. A belongings container marked with the patient's major incident number should be issued to each patient at triage.
- Communication: Most staff had mobile phones therefore internal communication was not a problem, but communication from hospital to MIO via Ambulance Incident Officer caused delay.
- Key staff must report to the HCC, but many enthusiastic members of staff and medical students rushed to the A&E and the area became crowded.

Acknowledgement

Mr Geoff Hinchley, Consultant in A&E at Chase Farm Hospital was co-author of the major incident plan for the Trust. The views expressed in this paper are based on my personal experience at Barnet Hospital.

Reference

1 Department of Health (1998, updated 2004) *Planning for major incidents: the NHS guidance.* DOH: London. www.dh.gov.uk/PublicationsAndStatistics/Publications/ PublicationsPolicyAndGuidance/PublicationsPolicyAndGuidanceArticle/fs/en?CONTENT _ID=4005419&chk=IWFhXF.

PART NINE

Patient focus

Chronic disease management: working together to improve patient care – the practice perspective

Roger Gadsby

Chronic disease management takes up much of the time of the general practitioner. It has been estimated that up to 80% of GP consultations involve chronic disease management. Sixty percent of adults over the age of 65 report that they have a long-term condition. The new GP contract QOF lists 10 chronic disease management areas, each with clinical indicators with attached points that can be achieved by meeting the indicators. The chronic disease areas are listed in Table A.

Table A   Ten chronic disease management areas

Clinical area	Points available
Secondary prevention in coronary heart disease	121
Stroke or transient ischaemic attack	31
Hypertension	105
Diabetes mellitus	99
Chronic obstructive pulmonary disease (COPD)	45
Epilepsy	16
Hypothyroidism	8
Cancer	12
Mental health	41
Asthma	72

Earning points means earning money, so there is a financial incentive for general practice teams to offer good quality chronic disease management. In my opinion the new contract QOF will be very significant in improving care.

Teamwork within practices

All members of the general practice team are involved in achieving high standards of care for people with chronic conditions:

- receptionists
- administrative staff (in my practice we have appointed a quality manager to oversee the new contract quality and outcomes framework)
- practice nurses
- GPs.

Skillmix

- Skillmix is changing within primary care with more work in chronic disease management being taken on by nurses. New roles for others are being opened up.
- Developing new roles, e.g. healthcare assistants.
- Using new skills, e.g. community pharmacists with supplementary prescribing qualifications to help with medication reviews in patients with chronic diseases.
- Enlisting the help of others, e.g. community dietitians, podiatrists, specialist nurses.

Practice example: diabetes

- Weekly diabetes clinic – run by practice diabetes nurse, supervised by GP partner.
- Insulin initiation – done by practice nurse supported by a diabetes specialist nurse (DSN).
- Monthly clinic – for those on insulin, or needing to go on insulin, run by practice diabetes nurse, community diabetes dietitian and DSN.

Practice example: asthma and COPD

Regular review of patients by practice nurses with an interest in asthma and COPD to do spirometry, checks on inhaler technique, develop patient management plans.

Education in chronic disease management

We need well-trained staff. Certificate, Diploma and Masters courses are available in diabetes, respiratory disease and coronary heart disease from a number of providers including the National Respiratory Centre, Warwick Diabetes Care and Heartsave. These three organisations are working together to provide a Diploma course in chronic disease management, which will be launched in 2005.

The nurse perspective: Diane James

Case management for chronic disease

The Kaiser three-level model of chronic disease management suggests that 70–80% of people with a chronic condition are at level 1. The smaller group of high-risk patients at level 2 require a care management approach and the very few highly complex patients at level 3 require a case management approach. It is in this latter group that significant reductions in emergency admissions to hospital have been demonstrated in the USA by using nurse case managers. These ideas are being developed in the UK, where nurses are proactively visiting and managing people with complex problems in order to try to reduce emergency admissions.

Self-mananagement for chronic disease

The cornerstone of chronic disease management is self-management, and the generic 'expert patient' programmes being rolled out across PCTs encourage the development of self-management skills in coping and dealing with the many facets of living with a chronic illness.

Good quality written materials to illustrate different aspects of chronic disease management can be very helpful in patient education.

The role of the clinician

Models of chronic disease management from the US emphasise that the clinician case manager needs to act as coach, champion, case orchestrator and communicator to achieve the aims of good management and to reduce the risk for the need for hospital admission.

The perspective of the community pharmacist with the supplemenary prescribing qualification

Community pharmacists have often in the past been overlooked when it comes to describing the team of healthcare professionals involved in caring for people with chronic diseases. However, they have a vital role to play in advising about the medications that people with chronic diseases need, and dispensing them.

Enhanced role: medication review in general practice

Pharmacists who have undertaken a six-month period of study and have successfully obtained the supplementary prescribing qualification are equipped to play a central role in the care of those with chronic diseases.

One way they can do this is through running medication review clinics in general practice. People with chronic diseases needing medication reviews and updates of their repeat prescriptions can see the pharmacist, who can check for drug interactions and side-effects, and review the effectiveness of therapy working within agreed protocols.

Enhanced role: medication review in care homes

People living in residential settings may often be taking a number of different medications. They may have impaired mobility and find it difficult to attend for practice-based repeat prescription checks. A community pharmacist with supplementary prescribing qualification can provide a service in the residential setting to do medication reviews, to check for side-effects, drug interactions and problems of compliance.

Evaluation of the Citizens Council of NICE

Elizabeth Barnett, Celia Davies, Margie Wetherell and Sarah Seymour-Smith

In accordance with *The NHS Plan 2000*[1], NICE set up a Citizens Council to deliberate on the social value judgements which underpinned its decisions. As the Citizens Council was an innovative initiative at national level, the NHS R&D Methodology Programme commissioned an evaluation of it.

Research design

The aim was to carry out an evaluation that would *provide information for policy-makers on how best to make use of citizens' time, when members of the public are invited to discuss complex issues*. It should *build on previous research in the area of public consultation to provide information for NICE on how to maximise value from the Citizens Council*. Six strands of work were specified:

1 a description of the process of recruitment and selection of participants
2 a description of the process and rationale of the selection of topics for deliberation
3 a description of how the topics were framed and the rationales for decisions
4 an assessment of how well participants felt supported and informed
5 a description of how the reports of the Council were produced and how they were received by NICE, its Board and relevant committees
6 an ethnographic study of the deliberations of the Council in session.

The evaluation was designed to provide a multi-method evaluation of the first stage of implementation of the Citizens Council, the core resource being devoted to an ethnographic study of interactions at its first four meetings. This sought to capture the details of actual practice in the Council meetings, which were recorded on videotape, transcribed and analysed using qualitative and quantitative measures of participation and influence to chart the trajectory of information and argument. It was complemented by an examination of Council members' perceptions. The original design proposed a combination of baseline interviews and repeated questionnaires with all the members (n = 30), augmented by data from four focus groups. Circumstances required that the questionnaires and focus groups be replaced by a second round of interviews following the third Council meeting. The third component of the evaluation focused on the evolution of policy and its organisational context. Drawing on the literature relevant to deliberative assemblies, it combined documentary analysis and semi-structured interviews with staff involved. Responding to the nature of the organisational modus operandi, this strand of the research evolved to encompass observation of Board and relevant committee meetings and workshops. The three aspects of the study were coordinated to explore best practice. NICE wanted this to be a formative as well as a summative evaluation. The research team therefore supplied both formal interim progress reports at four points over the duration of the study, and informal feedback and commentary as required in the interstices of Council meetings.

Since this was the first study to examine the reality of public deliberation in detail as it actually happens there were no pre-existing measures. A pragmatic empirical measure of deliberation was therefore adopted in terms of back-and-forth exchanges between two or more participants on the same topic. Additionally, drawing on the different literatures on deliberation, deliberative democratic models and public involvement we constructed two sets of evaluative criteria: for evaluating deliberative practice and for evaluating deliberative process. We also compiled a set of questions about participative advantage from other sources.

Results

We found a very successful recruitment and selection process produced a Council symbolically representative of the population of England and Wales. We also found that individual Council members benefited in terms of increased self-confidence, understanding of the dilemmas of healthcare, and interest in taking part in other arenas of public involvement. It was notable that discussion about social value judgements was also stimulated within NICE. However, creating an expertise space fit for the public proved a challenge and was only partially achieved by the fourth Council meeting. The empirical measure devised showed that no more than 25% of Council time was spent on actual deliberation.

Conclusions

This study is very relevant to patient and public involvement, which is a major current policy preoccupation. It demonstrates that:

1 given commitment and resourcing it is perfectly possible to stimulate the public's interest in participating in healthcare decision-making;

2   it is also possible to build the deliberative capital of participants by creating an expertise space in which they can contribute to decision-making optimally;

3   choosing concrete and meaningful topics, providing information in appropriate and accessible formats, facilitating inclusive practice in deliberating and communicating clearly the role and use of outputs are fundamental to achieving this. Health service organisations setting up deliberative public involvement initiatives need to prioritise these factors

4   further exploration of the complexities and potential contradictions involved in facilitating deliberation while maintaining inclusive practice is necessary. Practice is not well served by theory in this area.

Reference

1   Secretary of State for Health (2000) *The NHS Plan – a plan for investment, a plan for reform*. Department of Health: London.

Patients as drivers for implementation

Yvonne Boughton

FREED was established as a self-help group in 1996, the group registered with the Eating Disorders Association (EDA) and agreed to inform, encourage and support people with eating disorders and their carers and or families, attend training days, have regular supervision and attend EDA conferences; in return FREED could access EDA for information and advice. It very quickly became apparent that in our area there was no early intervention and no specialist help available until sufferers were at death's door.

Initially FREED applied for small grants to help the self-help group, e.g. £747 to purchase books and £3477 for a laptop and body image programme. The dietician/manager of the dietetic department at the Bassetlaw Hospital obtained a grant for herself, the child and family psychiatrist, and myself to travel to other specialist eating disorders services in order to decide on a service that we felt would be appropriate for Bassetlaw. The services visited were: St. George's, London (in-patient, Annex and Springfield children's unit); The Maudsley Institute Child and Family Therapy Unit (Chris Dare); The Phoenix Centre, Cambridge; The Juniper Centre, Southampton; and The Royal Free Hospital, London.

FREED was advised that success in achieving an ideal service was much more likely if a feasibility study was undertaken and comprehensive business plan and budget prepared; funding for this (£2500) was granted by The Charities Aid Foundation. To assist with the preparation of the business plan, FREED approached two local services: TANC (Technical Aid in Nottinghamshire Communities) and VOSE (Voluntary Organisations Support for Effective Management). Items to be included in the business plan were:

- one-page summary of the project (short, snappy and to the point)
- FREED's aims and objectives
- the project's aims and objectives
- a description of the project to be delivered
- an analysis of the need in the locality of the project
- statistics
- survey of other related services

- letters of support
- personal testimonies
- how the project would complement other services
- a work plan for the first year, including objectives, method of achievement and targets to be achieved in a set timetable
- details of monitoring achievement
- project management structure
- a detailed breakdown of costs, including capital and revenue
- a budget and cash-flow forecast, anticipated income and expenditure for the next three years
- a fundraising plan
- a marketing plan
- selling FREED and achievements to date
- staff requirements – job descriptions and job specifications.

After the research, including a questionnaire sent out to 150 sufferers (49 were returned; see Figure A), FREED decided that their ideal service would be as shown in Figure B.

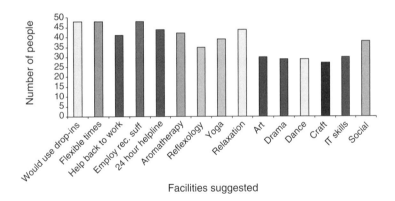

Figure A Bar chart to show from 49 people who returned our questionnaire how many would use each facility.

Evidence from the original self-help group showed that often help was sought very early in the illness either by carers or the person him/herself, but very rarely was any constructive help given until the person became extremely unwell. This service is aimed at offering specialist help right from early onset, aiming to assist with the psychological aspects of eating disorders working alongside the GP who monitors the physical well-being of the patient.

Having prepared the business plan and budget, FREED approached the four PCTs across North Notts to be told that they had no money for eating disorders.

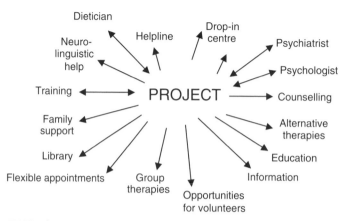

Figure B FREED's vision.

So the management committee decided to try to raise the funding from elsewhere. FREED was advised to become a registered charity as some funding is only available to registered charities. VOSE helped to prepare the constitution and FREED became registered charity number 1090776.

Funding was sought from several sources, some refused but the Lottery awarded a substantial amount (£159 356) along with Boots Plc, Barclays Bank, Lloyds TSB, Thomas Farr Trust and The Lady Hind Trust, all of which gave us the incentive to continue. Having secured much of the funding we returned to our PCTs, who agreed to contribute £10 000 each per year, which enabled the project to go ahead. FREED BEECHES (Bringing Empowerment Education, Counselling & Holistic Eating disorder Support) was up and running (funded to April 2006)!

FREED BEECHES is an innovative holistic centre, designed around service users' views, supporting people with eating disorders and the people who support them. The service offers an exceptional level of informality, intimacy, easy access and fast response in a homely environment. You are welcome to call in for a coffee and an informal chat before deciding whether to access the service.

We believe in offering the 'right help at the right time', beginning with a variety of self-help available, including manuals, books, CD-ROM programmes and self-help groups; if more than this is needed, we can offer a variety of counselling techniques, psychotherapy, complementary therapies and dietetic/nutrition advice. The service puts the patient first, which probably accounts for the very low number of patients who miss appointments; our DNA (did not attend) rate at the end of September was 1.6%. A success story for us is a young lady who had to come home from university because she was so frail. We offered to support her whilst her GP arranged inpatient treatment. She is still with us 8 months later, back at University part-time, has not had to have inpatient treatment, and the improvement is clear for all to see.

FREED BEECHES education programme includes talks to schoolchildren and colleges, taking information leaflets and a noticeboard to health fairs and training professionals around eating disorders. We believe passionately that early intervention, health promotion and education will alleviate suffering and free up more funding for other services. Our service is completely free thanks to our funders.

Barclays have funded a database for compiling much-needed quantitative statistics around eating disorders.

The NICE guidelines recommending early intervention, work with carers, self-help programmes, education and training have certainly helped our cause.

- Contact information: FREED BEECHES 39 Park Street, Worksop, Notts S80 1HW. Tel: +44 (0)1909 479922 Mon, Wed, Fri: 11.00am to 8.00pm (we are open on Saturdays by appointment). Email: info@freedbeeches.org.uk. Web: www.freedbeeches.org.uk.

Evaluating patient and carer involvement in NICE's Clinical Guidelines

Victoria Thomas

Background

In 2001, the National Institute for Clinical Excellence established the Patient Involvement Unit (PIU), a dedicated team providing strategic advice to NICE and its partner organisations on methods for involving patients and carers in the Institute's work programmes. The PIU's other key function is to provide (at an individual and organisational level) support, training, information and advice to the patients and carers involved in NICE's work.

Patients and carers have the opportunity to be involved in NICE's work at several levels. At a corporate level, there is lay representation on the Institute's Board and its Partners' Council. NICE also has a Citizens' Council, which is comprised of 30 members of the public. It provides the Institute with advice on issues of social value. At an organisational level, national bodies that represent the interests of patients and carers are able to take part in consultations on all of NICE's guidance products, from the initial scoping stage through to when the guidance is in draft form. Finally, each piece of guidance that NICE publishes is produced in a form specifically designed for patients, carers and members of the public.

NICE's clinical guidelines are produced by individually convened GDGs. These Groups are multidisciplinary and have as part of their membership at least two patient or carer members. The PIU facilitates an open and transparent process to recruit the patient and carer members. The patient and carer members of the GDGs are recruited to ensure that patients' and carers' perspectives inform the whole development process. The PIU was keen to evaluate the experiences of the patients and carers on the GDGs.

Methods

We conducted interviews with the patient and carer members and the Chairs from the first 20 GDGs. The interviews were initially conducted by staff from the PIU, and then by a freelance interviewer, using a semi-structured interview schedule. Both qualitative and quantitative data were collected. The study was slightly limited by the change of interviewer and minor changes to the interview schedule.

In total, 36 patient or carer Group members were interviewed, and 19 health professional Chairs. Of the patients and carers, 22 had direct personal experience of the condition being addressed by the guideline, and 5 were carers. Of these 27, 20 were also employees of patient/carer organisations. The data collected from the interviews was supplemented with written information from six patient/carer group members (from two different GDGs).

Schedule

We asked the patients, carers and Chairs similar questions, including:

- what their expectations were of being a member of a GDG (and in the case of the Chairs, also how they felt about having patients and carers as members of the Group)
- how they felt the Group had worked as a whole, and how it had been chaired
- what they thought of the support and training available
- their thoughts on the methodology used to develop the guideline
- what opportunities the patient/carer members had to contribute to the process, and what their actual contributions were
- their views on the final guideline and the 'information for the public' version of the guideline
- what their overall rating was of the experience.

What the patients and carers said

When we asked the patients and carers about their overall experience and their comments on the final guideline, almost without exception the responses were positive. People used words like 'good', 'enriching' and 'brilliant' to describe both the experience and the products. Their descriptions of their expectations of being involved in the project were quite mixed. Some people were very enthusiastic about the role they could play – 'I wanted to put the patient experience at the heart of the guideline' – while others were quite apprehensive: 'I was quite nervous even though I'm not a shy person'.

The patients and carers' experiences of being part of a multidisciplinary group were again predominantly positive, evidenced by quotes such as 'I was very welcomed by the group. It was an inclusive experience' and 'I felt that everything I was saying was being listened to … the group made a big effort'.

People's experiences of how well they felt the Groups had been chaired were quite varied, with people's comments ranging from 'I don't think we were dismissed by the Chair, but I don't think he had any desire to put the patient perspective forward' to '[the chair] did a brilliant job. He was a good facilitator; very inclusive'.

When asked about the scope and the methods used to develop the guideline, the responses were more negative than positive; with some people reflecting that the workload was often far greater than expected. One person said 'much of it was crisis management' and another described the methodology as 'not user-friendly'. In terms of training and support, in particular from the PIU, the comments were mostly encouraging, such as, 'they were excellent', but some people were not sure how the PIU fitted in with the other structures they were working with: 'I didn't understand the interaction'. We were pleased that most of the interviewees felt very positive about the impact they had had, 'providing a consistent voice on certain topics', and the potential for the guideline to have an influence on people's treatment saying that the guideline could 'potentially make a big difference to care'.

What the Chairs said

The Chairs were overwhelmingly enthusiastic about involving patients and carers in this process – 'it would have been unthinkable not to have them'; 'I would have been dismayed if they *hadn't* been part of the process' – but this contrasts with the mixed responses we had about the actual contributions that the patient/carer GDG members actually made. One Chair said, '[she contributed] nothing that made a difference to the weight of the guideline', while another was more positive saying, 'they gave a focus on the humanity of the topic'.

The Chairs had as many issues with the methodology as the patients and carers, in particular with the hierarchy of evidence. Their concerns were wide-ranging, from 'qualitative research doesn't figure in the hierarchy of evidence' to the broader problem that 'we spent 90% of our effort confirming what we know – that the research evidence base for this topic is very poor'. In terms of the impact that the patients and carers had on the final guidance products, again the responses were quite mixed. One chair said, 'without having a patient representative, we wouldn't have got such richness', while another thought 'she didn't make a difference'. Interestingly, one of the Chairs commented on the positive effect of having patients on the GDG, on the other health professionals on the Group: 'it created increased respect from the health professionals'.

Recommendations

As a result of the information that the participants gave us, we made several recommendations to try to improve the experience for future patient/carer GDG

members, some of which have already been implemented. These recommendations include:

- ensuring that due process is followed in terms of the recruitment of patient/
  carer members
- ensuring that the training offered by the PIU is systematic in its provision,
  aiming to give formal training as early as possible during the development
  of a guideline
- suggesting that each GDG meeting has a dedicated agenda item to discuss
  patients' and carers' concerns
- recruiting Chairs with good group facilitation skills and not necessarily
  clinical expertise
- where evidence on patients' views and experiences of treatment and care is
  lacking, commissioning dedicated initiatives to elicit these views
- establishing wide patient 'external reference groups' to sit alongside the
  GDGs and to act as a sounding board for the issues under discussion
- ensuring that there is a systematic search for qualitative information to
  incorporate into the evidence base
- developing consensus recommendations where evidence is lacking but
  where the issues are of importance, either clinically or from the patient's
  perspective.

Further information

Copies of the full evaluation report, describing our methods and results in detail,
are available from the PIU, or from the NICE website at www.nice.org.uk/
page.aspx?o = 216294.

- Contact details: Victoria Thomas, Assistant Director, Patient Involvement
  Unit, National Institute for Clinical Excellence, MidCity Place, 71 High
  Holborn, London WC1A 6NA. Tel: + 44 (0)20 7067 5861. Fax: + 44 (0)20
  7067 5801. Email: victoria.thomas@nice.nhs.uk.

Experience as a carer on the NICE self-harm guideline development group

Richard Pacitti

Many people seem to agree that involving patients and carers in the National Health Service (NHS) is a good idea. But how do we ensure that their input is meaningful? And that they are not just there to make up the numbers?

The Department of Health's Expert Patient Programme acknowledges that:

Many health professionals observe that 'my patient understands their disease better than I do'.

This knowledge and experience held by the patient has for too long been an untapped resource. It is something that could greatly benefit the quality of patients' care and ultimately their quality of life, but which has been largely ignored in the past.

DH, 2001

But what if, as in the case of self-harm, the guideline is not written for a clinical condition like cancer or asthma, but for a facet of human behaviour (albeit a behaviour that most people find perplexing, worrying or even shocking)? What if there isn't much academic evidence about what works and what doesn't? What if there is evidence, but not written in the way that fits into the conventional hierarchy of evidence? What if it's staff attitude and myths and misunderstandings that need to be addressed rather than clinical interventions?

People who self-harm and their carers can be reluctant to put themselves and their views forward because they know that the stigma and misunderstandings attached to self-harm will mean that they are often criticised, ignored or mistreated. In case you have any doubts about this, here are a couple of quotes from the newspapers following the launch of the guideline.

(People who self-harm) are so self-important that they think they have the right to clog up the NHS with their undeserving cases ... The nurses' attitude is understandable, given that they have to deal with genuine emergencies rather than the antics of a self-centred attention seeker.

Sunday Telegraph

It is hard not to get frustrated: people who self-harm do have a choice, although it may not seem like it at the time. They could not do it, or they could do it and stay at home to deal with the consequences. Just please don't lacerate yourself, come to hospital and then complain about it. A&E is an emergency service.

The Guardian

The hierarchy of evidence

NICE Clinical Guidelines work to a strict hierarchy of evidence thus:

Level	Type of evidence	Grade	Evidence
I	Evidence obtained from a single randomised controlled trial or a meta-analysis of randomised controlled trials	A	At least one randomised controlled trial as part of a body of literature of overall good quality and consistency addressing the specific recommendation (evidence level I) without extrapolation
IIa	Evidence obtained from at least one well-designed controlled study without randomisation	B	Well-conducted clinical studies but no randomised clinical trials on the topic of recommendation (evidence levels II or III); or extrapolated from level-I evidence
IIb	Evidence obtained from at least one other well-designed quasi-experimental study		
III	Evidence obtained from well-designed non-experimental descriptive studies, such as comparative studies, correlation studies and case studies		
IV	Evidence obtained from expert committee reports or opinions and/or clinical experiences of respected authorities	C	Expert committee reports or opinions and/or clinical experiences of respected authorities (evidence level IV). This grading indicates that directly applicable clinical studies of good quality are absent or not readily available

GPP	Recommended good practice based on the clinical experience of the GDG

Adapted from Eccles M and Mason J (2001) How to develop cost-conscious guidelines. *Health Technology Assessment.* **5**: 8; NHS Executive (1996) *Clinical Guidelines: Using Clinical Guidelines to improve patient care within the NHS.* NHSE, London.

In the self-harm GDG the service user and carer members were convinced that a search of the academic literature would not come up with much (we had spent years trawling through it). What we were aware of, though, was a very rich service user and voluntary sector literature, which gave ample evidence about how services could be improved for patients and their carers, as well as reducing the frustrations and difficulties faced by staff working with people who hurt themselves. Early on in the process it seemed that this evidence did not count because it was not in the academic literature and did not fit into the hierarchy of evidence.

There is evidence that other carers and patients in other GDGs had similar concerns.

In June 2004 the NICE Patient Involvement Unit published a report of a study evaluating patient/carer membership of the first NICE GDGs. The report showed that patient and carer members were worried that their views and experiences would be outweighed in the hierarchy of evidence.

> The methods ... are not user friendly. The need for high grade evidence is a real problem. People's experience should be given equal weight as the scientific evidence.
>
> NICE PIU, June 2004

Were our concerns justified? How did patient and carer views appear in the finished guideline?

In the NICE self-harm guideline the experience of people who self-harm, and how they experience services, was given the utmost priority. As part of the process a series of focus groups was arranged with service users. The recommendations they produced were very similar to those produced by the National Self-Harm Network in 1998: namely, that a non-judgemental approach be used, that they be treated the same as other patients using the NHS, that they receive adequate anaesthesia for wounds, that staff be trained in understanding self-harm, etc. The service user members submitted a paper entitled 'Ethical and good practice recommendations from patient representatives' emphasising similar points.

A reading of the key priorities for implementation from the self-harm guideline clearly shows how these views were reflected in it:

- People who have self-harmed should be treated with the same care, respect and privacy as any patient. In addition, healthcare professionals should take full account of the likely distress associated with self-harm.
- Clinical and non-clinical staff who have contact with people who self-harm in any setting should be provided with appropriate training to equip them to understand and care for people who have self-harmed.
- If a person who has self-harmed has to wait for treatment, he or she should be offered an environment that is safe, supportive and minimises any distress. For many patients, this may be a separate, quiet room with supervision and regular contact with a named member of staff to ensure safety.
- Adequate anaesthesia and/or analgesia should be offered to people who have self-injured throughout the process of suturing or other painful treatments.

Nearly all of the key recommendations in the guideline are at the 'good clinical practice' (GCP) level, largely based on the expertise of the members of the group (particularly patients and carers). The guideline also recommended more research and made major recommendations about the ongoing role of service users in the planning and commissioning of services, and in the future training of staff.

Index

Abacus International, NICE study 29–31
abbreviations xxi
ABPI perspective, NICE guidance 106–9
accountability
    CHRE role 77–80
    teams 77–80
    see also regulations/regulating
acetylcholinesterase inhibitors, ABPI
        perspective 107–8
Agenda for Change 141
Alzheimer's disease therapies, ABPI
        perspective 107–8
ambulance services, IPAS 95–8
appraisals, NICE 27–8, 87–90
arthritis, NICE guidance impact 112
assessment
    Healthcare Commission 32–6
    HTA 57–61, 87–90
    NICE guidance/guidelines 35
Assessment for improvement – Our approach,
        Healthcare Commission 32–3
asthma, chronic disease management 164
audit 73–6
    benefits 75
    costs 75
    effectiveness 75
    NICE guidance implementation 119–24

benefits
    audit 75
    R&D 17–19
beta interferon, NICE guidance impact 116,
        117
binge eating, psychological treatment 91–4
breast cancer, clinical trials 62–6
budgets/budgeting *see* funding
bulimia nervosa, psychological treatment
        91–4

cancer
    breast 62–6

challenge 13
clinical trials 62–6
colorectal 114
NICE guidance impact 114–16
NTRAC 15
opportunity 13–15
ovarian 114–16
research into practice 13–16
translational research 14–16
UKCRC 15
capecitabine, NICE guidance implementation
        120–1
carers, NICE guidance/guidelines 174–81
CBT *see* Cognitive Behaviour Therapy
challenges
    cancer 13
    R&D 17–19
Choosing Health: Making Healthier Choices 131
CHRE *see* Council for Healthcare Regulatory
        Excellence
chronic disease management
    diabetes therapies 164
    drugs 166
    education 165
    nurse perspective 165
    pharmacist perspective 166
    practice perspective 163–6
    skillmix 164
    teamwork 164–5
Citizens Council, evaluation, NICE 167–9
'click', dissecting room 145–6
clinical trials
    breast cancer 62–6
    cancer 62–6
    capacity 3–4
    Clinical Trials Toolkit 7
    EU Clinical Trials Directive 6–8
    HDA 10
    priorities 62–6
    websites 7
    see also R research

clinicians in risk management 154–6
clinicians' priorities, cancer clinical trials
    62–6
Cognitive Behaviour Therapy (CBT), eating
    disorders 91–4
colorectal cancer, NICE guidance impact
    114, 115
commercial potential 49–52
commissioning
    mental health quality 43–5
    mental health services 40–2
consent, obtaining 21–2
consultations, general practice 144–6
contract, nGMS *see* GMS contract
COPD, chronic disease management 164
costs
    audit 75
    see also funding
Council for Healthcare Regulatory
    Excellence (CHRE) 77–80
    functions 77–8
    teams, accountability 77–80
Cox II agents, NICE guidance impact 112
cromones, indication switching 49–52

diabetes therapies
    ABPI perspective 106–7
    chronic disease management 164
directives, EU Clinical Trials Directive 6–8
doctor–patient relationship 144–6
downstream interventions, HDA 10
drugs
    chronic disease management 166
    cromones 49–52
    indication switching 49–52
    NICE guidance implementation 119–24,
        141–3
    obesity 122
    potassium chloride/sodium chloride
        injections 141–3
    Roche 119–24
    safe medication guidance 141–3

eating disorders, psychological treatment
    91–4
economic responsibility, NICE 30
education, chronic disease management 165
ethics 20–3
    committees 20–3

    Helsinki Declaration 20–3
    Nuremberg Code 20–3
EU Clinical Trials Directive 6–8
    areas for further attention 7–8
    concerns 7
Evidence Briefings, HDA 9, 10
Evidence Reviews, HDA 9

falls, preventing 127–9
focus groups, PPP 18–19
FREED BEECHES, implementation 170–3
funding
    mental health 44–5
    R&D 3–5
future
    challenges 17–19
    NICE 29–31
    R&D 9–12, 17–19

General Dental Services 132
General Medical Services 131–2
    see also GMS contract
General Optical Services 133
General Pharmaceutical Services 132
general practice
    consultations 144–6
    dissecting room 'click' 145–6
    doctor-patient relationship 144–6
    generalist approach 144–5
    specialist approach 144–5
    see also GMS contract
glitazone therapies, ABPI perspective 106–7
glycoprotein IIB/III inhibitors, ABPI
    perspective 108
GMS contract 131–2
    benefits 132
    mental health 40–2
governance
    environment 6–8
    expectations 71–2
    R&D 69–72
    risk management 70–1
    see also regulations/regulating
growth hormone, NICE guidance impact
    116–17
guidance/guidelines, NICE *see* National
    Institute for Clinical Excellence
Guidance on Practice Based Commissioning,
    mental health 39

HDA *see* Health Development Agency
head injury guidance, NICE 103–5
health, determinants 130
Health Development Agency (HDA) 9–12
  downstream interventions 10
  Evidence Briefings 9, 10
  Evidence Reviews 9
  health inequalities 10
  products 9
  purpose 9
  research into practice 11
  social variations 10
  websites 9
health inequalities, HDA 10
Health Technology Assessment (HTA)
    87–90
  public involvement 57–61
Healthcare Commission 32–6
  assessment 32–6
  Assessment for improvement–Our approach
    32–3
  duties 32
  moving forward 36
  NICE guidance/guidelines 35
Helsinki Declaration, ethics 20–3
Herceptin® (trastuzumab) 14–16
  NICE guidance implementation 120–1
hierarchy of evidence, NICE guidance/
    guidelines 179–80
hospitals
  major incidents 157–60
  smokefree 134–7
HTA *see* Health Technology Assessment

implementing NICE guidelines *see* National
    Institute for Clinical Excellence
implementing R&D 17–19
Improvement Partnership for Ambulance
    Services (IPAS) 95–8
incidents, major, hospitals 157–60
indication switching, drugs 49–52
inequalities, health, HDA 10
inter-professional learning 80
interventional procedures
  Leicester experience 152–3
  local implementation 147–51
  new 147–51, 152–3
  NICE 27–8
  NIPAG 152–3

regulations 150
  safety 152–3
involving patients/carers, NICE guidance/
    guidelines 174–81
involving public, HTA 57–61
IPAS *see* Improvement Partnership for
    Ambulance Services
irinotecan, NICE guidance impact 114, 115

James Lind Alliance 49–66

learning, multi/inter-professional 80
legal issues *see* governance; regulations/
    regulating
Leicester experience, new interventional
    procedures 152–3
Local Research Ethics Committees (LRECs)
    20–3

MabThera (rituximab), NICE guidance
    implementation 122
major incidents, hospitals 157–60
medications *see* drugs
mental health
  funding 44–5
  Guidance on Practice Based Commissioning
    39
  quality, commissioning 43–5
  services, commissioning 39–42
motor neurone disease, NICE guidance
    impact 113–14
Multi-centre Research Ethics Committees
    (MRECs) 20–3
multiple sclerosis, NICE guidance impact
    116, 117

National Cancer Research Institute (NCRI)
    15
National Cancer Tissue Resource 15
National Institute for Clinical Excellence
    (NICE) 27–31
  Abacus International 29–31
  ABPI perspective 106–9
  aims 27
  appraisals 27–8, 87–90
  assessment 35
  audit 119–24
  Citizens Council evaluation 167–9
  economic responsibility 30

future 29–31
guidance/guidelines assessment 35
guidance/guidelines basis 28–9
guidance/guidelines development 81–4,
    85–124
guidance/guidelines forms 27–8
guidance/guidelines hierarchy of evidence
    179–80
guidance/guidelines impact 110–18
guidance/guidelines implementation 29–
    31, 85–124, 119–24, 141–3, 170–3
guidance/guidelines involvement,
    patients/carers 174–81
guidance/guidelines principles 28–9
head injury guidance 103–5
Healthcare Commission 35
HTA 87–90
interventional procedures 27–8
methodologies 29
pressure ulcer guidance 99–102
programmes 27
public health responsibility 30–1
self-harm guidance 178–81
stakeholders' impact 81–4
National Patient Safety Agency (NPSA)
    154–6
NCRI see National Cancer Research Institute
New Interventional Procedures Advisory
    Group (NIPAG) 152–3
nGMS contract see GMS contract
NHS
    R&D 3–5
    reforms, 1990; 73–6
    structural issues, R&D 69–72
NICE see National Institute for Clinical
    Excellence
NIPAG see New Interventional Procedures
    Advisory Group
NPSA see National Patient Safety Agency
NTRAC, cancer 15
Nuremberg Code, ethics 20–3
nurse perspective, chronic disease
    management 165
nutrition, older people 127–9

obesity drugs, NICE guidance
    implementation 122
obesity surgery, NICE guidance impact 111–
    12

older people
    nutrition 127–9
    preventing falls 127–9
opportunity, cancer 13–15
orlistat, NICE guidance implementation
    122–3
ovarian cancer, NICE guidance impact
    114–16
oxaliplatin, NICE guidance impact 114,
    115

partnerships, PPP 18–19
patients
    doctor–patient relationship 144–6
    focus 161–81
    as implementation drivers 170–3
    NICE guidance/guidelines 174–81
    perspectives, psoriasis 53–6
    priorities, cancer clinical trials 62–6
    safety 141–60
Pegasys, NICE guidance implementation
    123
pegylated interferons, NICE guidance
    implementation 123
pegylated liposomal doxorubicin
    hydrochloride (PLDH), NICE guidance
    impact 114–16
pharmacist perspective, chronic disease
    management 166
PLDH see pegylated liposomal doxorubicin
    hydrochloride
potassium chloride/sodium chloride
    injections 141–3
PPP see Private Public Partnership
practice perspective
    chronic disease management 163–6
    teamwork 164–5
practice, research into 11, 13–16
pressure ulcer guidance, NICE 99–102
primary care
    public health 130–3
    quality 130–3
priorities
    cancer clinical trials 62–6
    research 49–66
Private Public Partnership (PPP) 18–19
psoriasis
    patients' perspectives 53–6
    research 53–6

psychological treatment, eating disorders
    91–4
public health
    defining 130
    primary care 130–3
    quality 125–37, 130–3
public health responsibility, NICE 30–1
public involvement, HTA 57–61

QOF *see* Quality and Outcomes Framework
quality
    achieving 125–37
    commissioning, mental health 43–5
    primary care 130–3
    public health 125–37, 130–3
Quality and Outcomes Framework (QOF)
    131–2

R&D 3–23
    Abacus International 29–31
    areas 3–5
    benefits 17–19
    challenges 17–19
    directorate 69–70
    focus 9–12
    funding 3–5
    future 9–12, 17–19
    governance 69–72
    implementing 17–19
    NHS 3–5
    NHS structural issues 69–72
    reports 3–4
    types 3
    UKCRC 4–5
    see also clinical trials; research
raltitrexed, NICE guidance impact 114
randomised controlled trials (RCTs) *see*
    clinical trials
Reductil (sibutramine), NICE guidance
    implementation 122–3
reforms, 1990, NHS 73–6
regulations/regulating
    areas for further attention 7–8
    CHRE 77–80
    concerns 7
    environment 6–8
    individuals vs. teams 79
    interventional procedures 150
    see also accountability; governance

research
    cancer 13–16
    governance 69–72
    HDA 11
    into practice 11, 13–16
    priorities 49–66
    psoriasis 53–6
    translational 14–16
    see also clinical trials; R&D
riluzole, NICE guidance impact 113–14
risk management
    clinicians in 154–6
    research governance 70–1
    see also safety
rituximab, NICE guidance implementation
    122
Roche drugs
    audit 119–24
    NICE guidance implementation 119–24

safety
    consultations 144–6
    interventional procedures 152–3
    major incidents, hospitals 157–60
    NPSA 154–6
    patients 141–60
    safe medication guidance 141–3
    see also risk management
self-harm guidance, NICE guidance
    implementation 178–81
services, commissioning, mental health 39–
    42
sibutramine, NICE guidance implementation
    122–3
Slamon, Dr Dennis 14
Smith, Richard 27
smokefree hospitals 134–7
social variations, HDA 10
sodium chloride/potassium chloride
    injections 141–3
somatropin, NICE guidance impact 116–17
stakeholders' impact, NICE guidance/
    guidelines development 81–4

teams
    accountability, CHRE 77–80
    regulations/regulating 77–80
    translational research 14
teamwork, practice perspective 164–5

technology *see* Health Technology
    Assessment
topotecan, NICE guidance impact 114–16
translational research
    cancer 14–16
    defining 14
    importance 15–16
    NCRI 15
    teams 14
    UK solution 15
trastuzumab 14–16
    NICE guidance implementation 120–1

UK Clinical Research Collaboration (UKCRC)
    cancer 15

guiding principles 4–5, 8
    R&D 4–5
ulcer guidance, NICE 99–102

ViraferonPeg®, NICE guidance
    implementation 123

websites
    Clinical Trials Toolkit 7
    HDA 9

Xeloda (capecitabine), NICE guidance
    implementation 120–1
Xenical (orlistat), NICE guidance
    implementation 122–3